THE GOLD GUIDES

VIENNA

A VISITOR'S GUIDE TO THE CITY

D1795172

BONECHI VERLAG STYRIA

Vertrieb
für Österreich
VERLAG STYRIA
Schönaugasse 64
A-8010 GRAZ

für Deutschland
Butzon & Bercker GmbH
Hooge Weg 71
D-47623 Kevelaer

für die Schweiz
Herder AG Basel
Muttenzerstraße 109
CH-4133 Pratteln 1

Publication created and designed by: Casa Editrice Bonechi
Editorial management: Monica Bonechi
Iconographic research, graphic design and layout: Sonia Gottardo
Video page-making: Laura Settesoldi
Cover: Manuela Ranfagni
Editing: Anna Baldini

Translation: Paula Boomsliter

Maps edited by the Casa Editrice Bonechi editorial staff.

Drawings: Stefano Benini

© Copyright by Casa Editrice Bonechi - Florence - Italy
E-mail:bonechi@bonechi.it - Internet:www.bonechi.it

Printed in Italy by Centro Stampa Editoriale Bonechi.

The photographs are property of the Casa Editrice Bonechi Archives, with the
exception of

Bildarchiv der Österreichischen Nationalbibliothek: *p. 52 top.*
Bundesministerium für Land- und Forstwirtschaft: *pp. 50 bottom, 51.*
Historisches Museum der Stadt Wien: *pp. 5, 17, 21 bottom, 27 bottom, 28 bottom,*
29 top, 38, 49 bottom, 56 top, 59 upper right, 106.
Kunsthistorisches Museum Wien: *pp. 4, 6, 71, 72 top, 80, 87 upper left.*
Museum für Angewandte Kunst (Photo Gerald Zugmann): *p. 99 top.*
Naturhistorisches Museum Wien: *pp. 72 bottom, 73.*
Wiener Tourismusverband: *p. 109.*

ISBN 3-222-12596-1

* * *

Historical Overview

Vienna and the surrounding territory have been inhabited since the Neolithic Age. At the crossroads of the most heavily-travelled European highways (the crossing of the Alps, the Danube river, the Amber Route) there arose an Illyrian-Celtic settlement called Vindobona *(on the site of today's Leopoldsberg); the Romans, who reached the Danube in 15 BC, established a military camp of the same name on the south bank of the river. This included a part of what is today the first* Bezirk *(district), approximately delimited by Tiefer Graben - Naglergasse - Graben - Kramergasse - Rotgasse. The village was instead located on the site of what is now the third* Bezirk *(Rennweg, Aspangbahnhof). Both were destroyed in 166 AD during the Marcomanni invasion. The military city of Vindobona, rebuilt and re-fortified, was the headquarters of the Roman Emperor Marcus Aurelius in his campaigns against the Germanic tribes and the probable site of his death in 180. When the Roman frontier along the Danube fell in the 5th century, Vindobona was*

The siege of Vienna of 1683. Detail of a painting by Georg Philipp Rugendas.

Empress Maria Theresa in a painting by Martin van Meytens.

again ravaged; there remained only a small, barbarized settlement. A Longobard cemetery on Viennese territory indicates that Vindobona was at one time under the influence of this Germanic people, who were probably preceded by the Goths, the Alani and the Rugi. By the end of the 6th century there had been created in the Vienna area a power vacuum into which the Avars and the Slav tribes advanced.

The centuries that followed were Vienna's darkest times: there exists no mention of the city, the environs of which were colonized by the Frankish Bavarians after Charlemagne's victory over the Avars in 796 AD. The names of the patron saints of the oldest churches in Vienna (Ruprecht, Peter) show that there existed relations with the Bavarian Missionary Center of Salzburg. Even the name Vindobona (or Vindomina) disappeared during the period of the city's decline: in the first medieval mention (881), the city is called Wenia (from the Celtic Vedunia - «woodland stream»). Vienna thus takes its modern name from that small tributary (today called the Donaukanal) which from the Viennese wood flows from west to east through the city to empty into the Danube. In the 10th century the city was controlled by the Hungarian nomads, who nevertheless did not interfere with the process of Franco-Bavarian colonization. At that time only a part of the Vienna enclosed by the ancient Roman walls was populated: the so-called Berghof (Hoher Markt - Marc Aurelstrasse) was probably a fortified center, while rural settlements had grown up around the churches of Saint Ruprecht and Saint Peter. Vienna, enfeoffed to the German Babenbergs as early as 976, had by the year 1000 become the easternmost Bavarian March. Although the city was mentioned in 1030 in relation to the military action undertaken by the Emperor Conrad against the Hungarians, it remained in the shadows with respect to other cities on the Danube such as Melk, Krems, Tulln and Klosterneuburg. But in the 12th century Vienna began a new and rapid climb to glory: Austria was elevated to the rank of Grand Duchy in 1156 and the first Duke Heinrich II (called Jasomirgott) chose Vienna as his residence (Herzogliche Burg am Hof). By the year 1200, Vienna was the most densely-populated and most economically-important German city after Cologne. The first Stadtrecht (city rights proclamation), dating to 1221, is an expression of this status. The extensive political relations woven by the Babenbergs procured many advantages for Vienna, and the city soon became the meeting-place of different cultural influxes. Lively contacts with Flemish, Walloon and English circles contrasted with relations

Emperor Joseph II in a painting by Joseph Hickel (1771).

The panorama of Vienna from the Belvedere, in a painting
by Bernardo Bellotto (1759/60).

with Byzantium, Bohemia and Hungary: the Viennese court of
the Babenbergs also became one of the nuclei of aulic culture.
By the early 13th century, successive enlargements had brought
the city to the size it was to remain until the 19th century (corre-
sponding approximately to the extension of the first Bezirk).
After the extinction of the Babenberg dynasty in 1246, Vienna
found itself involved in the disputes over their legacy but main-
tained the status of Ducal Residence after the Hapsburgs took
over Austria in 1282. The late Middle Ages saw the flowering of
the Gothic Vienna (the Hofburg as new Residence, the Stephansdom, Maria am Gestade); the city's position as a political and
cultural center was consolidated under Duke Rudolf IV with the
founding of the University of Vienna in 1365. Latent dissention
marked relations between the rich and haughty bourgeoisie and
ducal government; Vienna was more than once forced to take a
stance in the internal disputes of the Hapsburgs, and in 1462 it
did not hesitate to lay siege to Emperor Friedrich III in the Hofburg. From 1485 to 1490, it was occupied by King Matthias
Corvinus of Hungary. Maximilian I inspired a revival of the hu-
manistic spirit of the University, but preferred Innsbruck to Vienna for his residence. His policies toward Burgundy and Spain
brought no direct advantages to Vienna, but relations between
the city and the East were reinforced through the Congress of
Princes and the double wedding of 1515.
The greater degree of independence from the Hapsburgs
achieved by Vienna during these years was lost in the attempt to
consolidate it: the exponents of the tyrannical council were exe-

cuted in Wiener Neustadt (1522). From then on, Vienna assumed a clearly Imperial aspect, although it periodically shared its role as Imperial Residence with Graz and Innsbruck, which had also come under Hapsburg domination. The takeover of Bohemia in 1526 led to conflict with Prague, which became the temporary seat of the Hapsburgs (above all under Emperor Rudolf II).

As early as the 16th century, Vienna was considered as being the «Heart and Shield» of the Germanic Holy Roman Empire. This honorary title was granted to the city in recognition of its role as the eastern bulwark of defense against the aggressive Islamic Ottoman Empire: in 1529 and again in 1683, Vienna was in fact besieged by the Turks. After the aggressors had been vanquished for the second time, splendid Baroque buildings sprang up all over Vienna, and in the city itself as well as in the surrounding areas supplanted many Gothic constructions. During the reigns of Karl VI, Maria Theresa and Joseph II, Vienna became one of the most important cities in the world: currents from East and West, North and South mingled to create in the city a multi-faceted cultural life. The Congress of Vienna (1814-1815), during which the new European order following the Napoleonic Wars was decided, made the city the resplendent capital of Europe.

In the years that followed, however, there surfaced the first crises that were destined to undermine the social and economic structure of the city. The Biedermeier culture, closely linked to Vienna's middle classes, widened the fissures in the political fabric of Austrian society as a whole and in particular in the city of the Imperial Residence. Although the revolution of March 1848 forced the Emperor to flee Vienna, it nevertheless failed due to conflicts from within between radicals and moderate democrats: Vienna was re-taken by the Imperial army. Demolition of the city walls began under Emperor Franz Joseph I, as did construction of the Ringstrasse (ring-road), lined with sumptuous buildings that are still today kept up in their original style, and annexation to the City of Vienna of suburbs (today the II-IX Bezirks) and other outlying areas (today the X-XIX Bezirks). In the years separating 1848 and 1918, massive immigration from every corner of the Hapsburg Empire determined an increase in the population from 440,000 to 2,200,000 inhabitants. Heavy industrialization took place to the south and the west of the city and entire workers' neighborhoods arose, characterized by miserable hovels. The social and economic problems in the fields of national insurance and urban modernization and rationalization were tackled through wide-ranging actions by city government. And this, together with the expansion of artistic and scientific activity that the city enjoyed during those decades, made Vienna a true metropolis. With the downfall of the Hapsburg Empire in 1918, Vienna became the capital of a small, torn-apart country and was disparagingly termed the «Wasserkopf» (swelled head) of the new Republic: more than one-quarter of all Austrians live in Vienna! Despite all the crises and internal conflicts, the city has preserved its status as the hub of culture. The exemplary actions taken by the City of Vienna, especially in the field of public housing, have earned the admiration of the entire international community. The civil uprising of 1934 was damaging to the development of Vienna, as was the loss of its role as capital in 1938 despite the expansion of the city (Gross-Wien). Vienna suffered

Emperor Franz Joseph I in a painting by Franz Winterhalter (1865).

Empress Elizabeth in a painting by Franz Winterhalter (1865).

heavy damage from Allied bombings and again in April 1945, when it became a battle-ground. The city remained split into four zones until 1955, but despite censorship and the severe surveillance that hobbled public life it was possible to rebuild the sorely-tried city. Since 15 May 1955, when the Austrian State Treaty was signed at the Upper Belvedere, Vienna has been the capital of the neutral Austrian Federal Republic (Bundesrepublik Österreich). The area on the north bank of the Danube (Floridsdorf, Donaustadt) has drawn attention in the last few decades, since it is here that UNO-City, headquarters of a number of United Nations organizations, now arises. Since 1979, Vienna has been the third United Nations city, after New York and Geneva.

Georg Scheibelreither

8 ITINERARIES THROUGH VIENNA

We have divided the panorama of artistic, cultural and historical attractions offered by the City of Vienna into 8 different itineraries, each of which may be completed in a morning's or an afternoon's time.

Each walk will take the tourist through the one of most interesting areas of the city; the guide points out the most famous monuments, churches, museums and patrician homes as well as little-known facts and the typical and singular aspects of each.

The sights that must absolutely not be missed are printed in boldface for easy reference by the especially harried tourist.

I - p. 14

Stephansdom (Saint Stephan's Cathedral) - Stephansplatz (Saint Stephan's Square) - **Graben** - **«Am Hof»** - Uhrenmuseum (Clock Museum) - **Freyung** - Schottenkirche (Scottish Church) - Freyung-Passage.

II - p. 34

Michaelerplatz - **Hofburg** - Michaelertrakt - **Kaiserappartements** (State Apartments) - **«In der Burg»** - Amalienburg - Leopoldinischer Trakt - Reichskanzleitrakt - Alte Burg - Burgkapelle (Imperial Chapel) - **Weltliche und Geistliche Schatzkammer** (Sacred and Secular Treasuries) - Heldenplatz - Neue Burg - Neue Hofburg Museums - Hofburg Gardens - Stallburg - Josefsplatz - Nationalbibliothek (National Library) - **Spanische Hofreitschule** (Spanish Riding School) - Augustinerkirche (Augustine Church) - Albertina.

III - p. 54

Staatsoper - Hotel Sacher - **Kärntnerstrasse** - **Kaisergruft** (Imperial Crypt) - Stadtpalais des Prinzen Eugen (Winter Palace of Prince Eugene) - Franziskanerkirche (Franciscan Church) - Figarohaus (House of Figaro) - Dominikanerkirche (Dominican Church) - Schönlaterngasse - Heiligenkreuzerhof - Bernhardskapelle (Chapel of Saint Bernard) - Jesuitenkirche (Jesuit Church) - Akademie der Wissenschaften (Academy of Sciences) - Alte Universität - **Hoher Markt** - **Altes Rathaus** - Böhmische Hofkanzlei - Judenplatz - **Maria am Gestade** (Church of Saint Mary on the Bank) - Fleischmarkt - **Ruprectskirche** (Church of Saint Ruprecht).

IV - p. 66

Ringstrasse - Äusseres Burgtor - Maria-Theresien-Platz - Messepalast (Exhibition Palace) - **Kunsthistorisches Museum** (Museum of the History of Art) - Naturhistorisches Museum (Museum of Natural History) - Parliament - Pallas-Athene-Brunnen (Fountain of Athena Pallas) - **Burgtheater** - **Rathaus** (City Hall) - Rathauspark - Universität - Votivkirche - Minoritenplatz - Minoritenkirche (Church of the Friars Minor).

V - p. 78

Schloss Schönbrunn (Schönbrunn Castle) - **Kaiserliche Appartements** (Imperial Apartments) - **Park** - Botanischer Garten (Botanical Garden) - Palmenhaus (Palm House) - **Wagenburg** (Imperial Coach Museum) - Technisches Museum (Technical Museum).

VI - p. 88

Unteres Belvedere (Lower Belvedere) - Österreichisches Barockmuseum (Museum of Austrian Baroque Art) - **Belvedere Park** - **Oberes Belvedere** (Upper Belvedere) - Österreichische Galerie des 19. und 20. Jahrhunderts (Museum of 19th- and 20th-Century Art) - Stadtpark - Kursalon - Wienflussportal (Portal of the River Wien) - **Museum für Angewandte Kunst** (Austrian Museum of Applied Arts) - Postsparkasse (Austrian Post Office Savings Bank) - Urania - **Prater**.

VII - p. 102

Karlskirche (Church of Saint Charles Borromeo) - Karlsplatz - **Historisches Museum der Stadt Wien** (Historical Museum of the City of Vienna) - Musikvereinsgebäude (Society of the Friends of Music Building) - Künstlerhaus (Artists' House) - Historische Stadtbahnstationen (Historical Underground Pavilions) - **Sezession** (Sezession Building) - Akademie der Bildenden Künst (Academy of Fine Arts) - **Linke Wienzeile** - Theater an der Wien - Naschmarkt - Flohmarkt (Flea Market) - Majolikahaus - Spittelberg - Barockhaus am Ulrichsplatz - Bäckereimuseum (Bakery Museum) - Piaristenkirche Maria Treu (Piarist Church) - Palais Liechtenstein - Museum für Moderne Kunst (Museum of Modern Art) - Josephinum - Sigmund Freud-Haus.

VIII - p. 114

Museum des 20. Jahrhunderts (Museum of the Twentieth Century) - **Heeresgeschichtliches Museum** (Museum of Army History) - Hundertwasserhaus - **St. Marxer Friedhof** (Saint Marx Monumental Cemetery) - **Zentralfriedhof** (Central Cemetery) - Kirche am Steinhof - Karl Marx-Hof - UNO-City (United Nations City) - Donaupark - Heurigen.

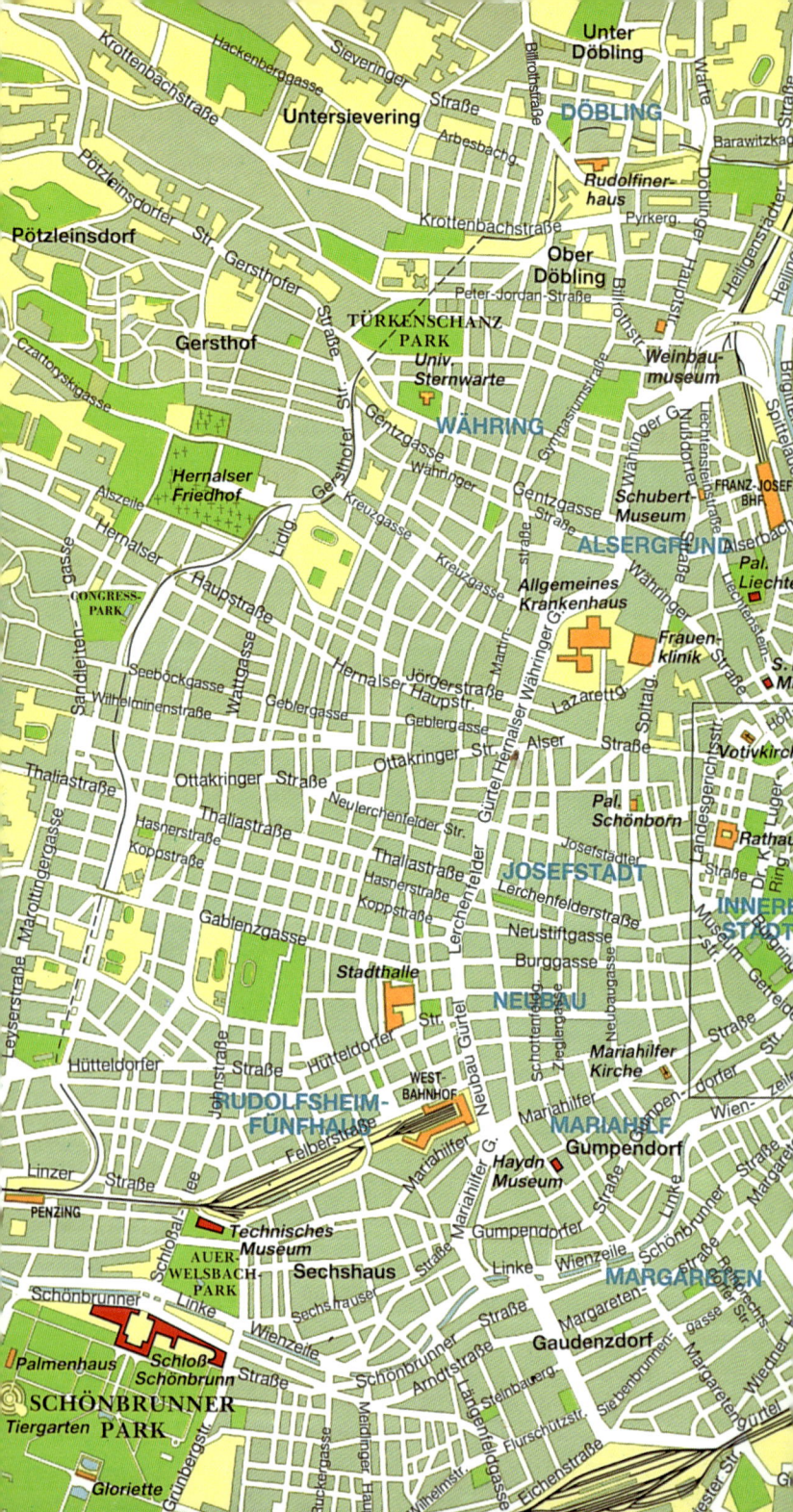

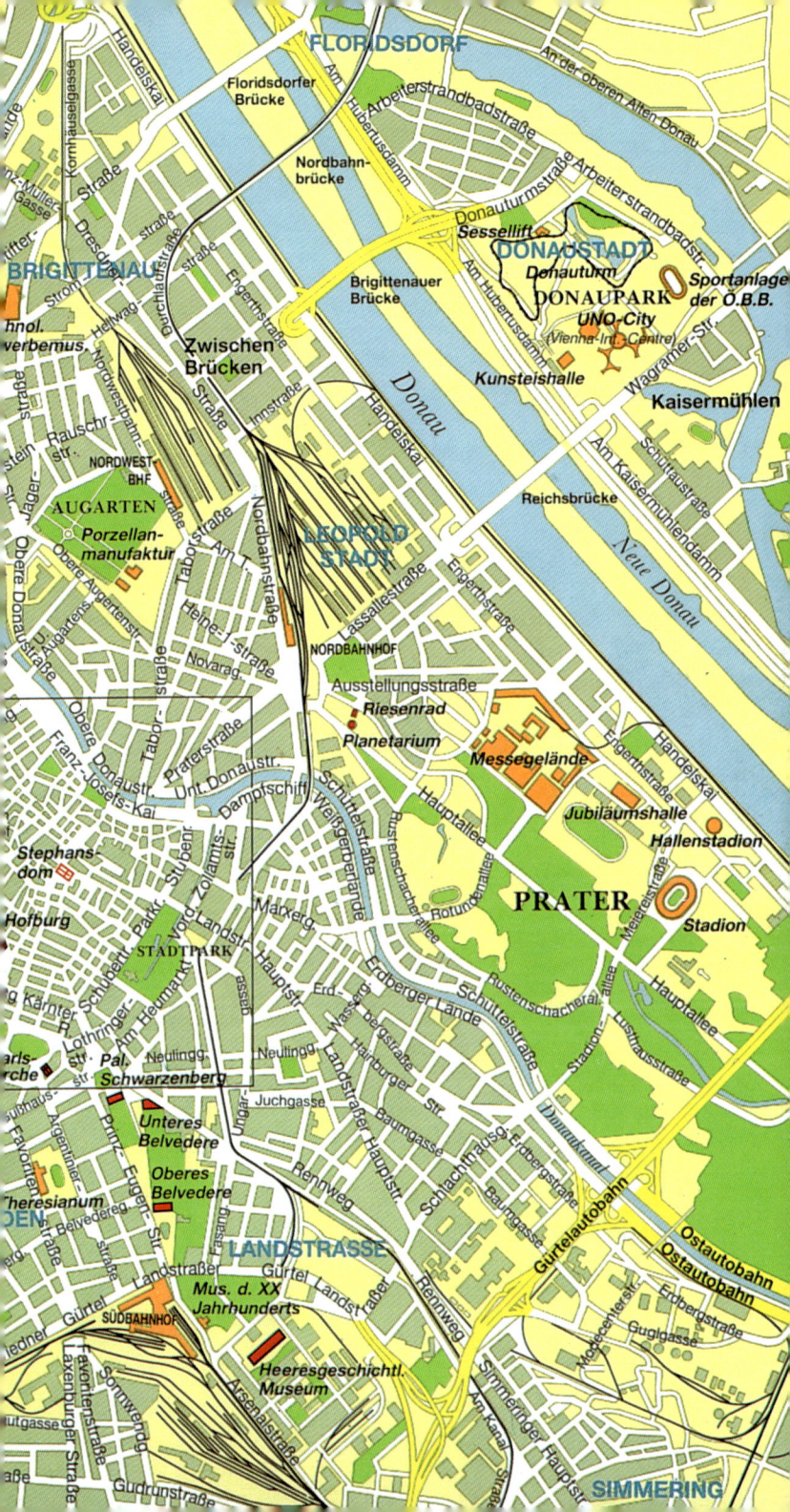

Palais Daun-Kinsky • 31, 32

The Scottish Church • 32, 33

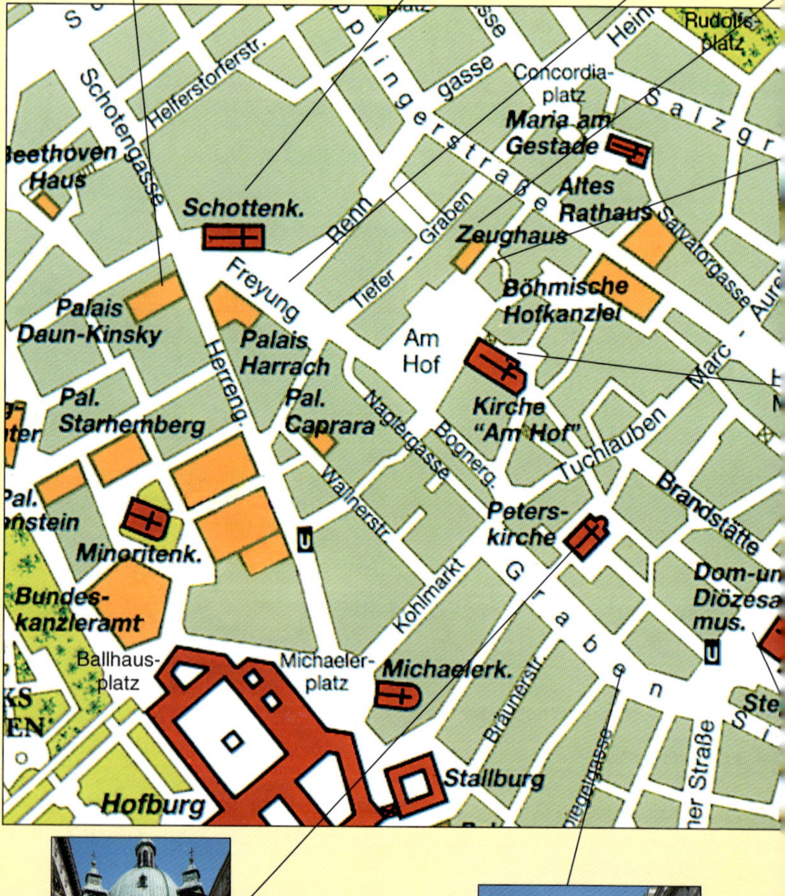

*The Freyung and the
Freyung-Passage
• 32, 33*

Schottenk.

Palais
Daun-Kinsky

Palais
Harrach

Pal.
Caprara

Pal.
Starhemberg

Pal.
nstein

Minoritenk.

Bundes-
kanzleramt

Ballhaus-
platz

Michaeler-
platz

Hofburg

Stallburg

Freyung

Herreng.

Wallnerstr.

Kohlmarkt

Naglergasse

Michaelerk.

Bräunerstr.

Beethoven
Haus

Schotengasse

Helferstorferstr.

Renng.

Concordia-
platz

Maria am
Gestade

Altes
Rathaus

Zeughaus

Böhmische
Hofkanzlei

Am
Hof

Kirche
"Am Hof"

Peters-
kirche

Tuchlauben

Brandstätte

Dom-un
Diözesa
mus.

Ste

Graben

Tiefer - Graben

Salzgr

Salvatorgasse

Marc - Aure

Bogner g.

Rudolfs
platz

Hein

plingerstra

gasse

platz

Peterskirche • 28, 29

The Graben • 27/29

The Zeughaus, once the city arsenal • 30, 31

Stephansdom (Saint Stephan's Cathedral) - Stephansplatz (Saint Stephan's Square) - **Graben** - **«Am Hof»** - Uhrenmuseum (Clock Museum) - **Freyung** - Schottenkirche (Scottish Church) - Freyung-Passage.

The Clock Museum • 31, 32

«Am Hof» • 29/32

Stephansdom • 16/25

Stephansplatz, the Cathedral and Diocesan Museum • 26

STEPHANSDOM

In the third decade of the 12th century, the Bishop of Passau ordered construction of the first Romanesque parish church on the site. Consecrated by him in 1147, it was a little smaller than the nave of today's cathedral. Rebuilding was delayed on account of the fire that devastated the city in 1258 and was completed only in 1263, during the Interregnum. Albrecht I, son of Rudolf of Hapsburg, began construction of the Gothic choir (1304-1340) as it appears today. The first stone of the Gothic nave was laid in 1359 by Rudolf IV the

The Stephansdom seen from the Graben.

Founder, while the South Tower, completed in 1433, was being built. Work on the North Tower, which was never completed, continued from 1450 through 1511. In 1469, under Emperor Friedrich III, Vienna became a bishopric and the Stephansdom the diocesan church. The various 17th-century reconstructions in Baroque style did not succeed in radically altering the original Gothic aspect of the Cathedral.

In April 1945, during the last days of World War II, the Stephansdom caught fire during bombing. Long and painstaking restoration work, carried out thanks to funding provided by all the Austrian regions and terminated only in 1956, re-

The Stephansdom seen from the north in an engraving by Carl Schütz.

The Stephansdom with the two Heidentürme (Heathen Towers). Facing page: the tympanum of the Singertor (Singers' Gate).

turned the Cathedral all its ancient splendor.

The massive, compact form of the Cathedral, with an external length of 107 meters and a height at the roof ridge of 60 meters, is softened by the two Heidentürme. The splendid colored tile roof, which was originally supported by larch wood beams and was completely destroyed in 1945, has been rebuilt in steel.

West Facade - The **Riesentor** (Giants' Doorway) and the two compact side towers, called the **Heidentürme** (Heathen Towers) are all that remain of the original Romanesque church. The Riesentor is decorated with geometrical figures, animal motifs and the images of saints. Special mention must be made of the small figures in the left-hand corner: the *Steinmetz* (stone-cutter) and *Saint Peter* bearing a large key. In the tympanum is a *Seated Christ* with His left knee uncovered, a book in His hand and two angels at the sides. This sculpted relief has been the subject of much discussion among art historians, some of whom argue that the uncovered knee alludes to the Masonic rite by which new initiates participated in the ceremony with their knee bared. On the facade are also found Romanesque sculptures, including, to the right of the doorway, a griffin and *Samson and the Lion*. To the right of the Riesentor we note the number «05», carved here in 1945 to symbolize the Austrian Resistance Movement against National Socialism and an-

Christ Imparting the Blessing. Detail of the Reisentor (Giants' Doorway).

nexation of Austria to Hitler's Germany. The number 5 signifies the fifth letter of the alphabet, and therefore 05 = OE = Oesterreich.

Exterior - On the right of the Cathedral (south side) is the **Singertor** (Singers' Gate), by Hans Puchsbaum, with a Gothic portal dating to 1440-1445. This door, decorated with many statues and sculpted reliefs, is comparable to the Riesentor for beauty. To the right, a niche contains the *statue of Rudolf IV the Founder* holding in his hand a model of the choir (built between 1304 and 1340) with the two planned towers.

The statue of Rudolf IV the Founder on the Singertor, and the relief sculptures on the Reisentor.

Further ahead, we come to the Baroque Untere Sakristei (Lower Sacristy) over which there rises the slender, extremely aesthetic South Tower (**«Steffl»** , as it is affectionately called by the Viennese). One-hundred and thirty six meters in height, the many-spired tower is a highly valuable masterpiece of Gothic architecture and owes its elegant form to its peculiar structure: the tower, as it rises from the square base, becomes octagonal. Inside, a spiral staircase of 343 steps

leads to the so-called Türmerstube (Bell-Ringer's Room) from which we may enjoy a splendid view of the city.

All around the apse of the church are 15th- and 16th-century reliefs as well as a number of statues and the 15th-century **Capistrankanzel** (Capistrano Pulpit) from which Saint Johannes Capistrano preached in favor of a crusade against the Turks in 1451. The 15th-century statue of the *Schmerzensmann* (Ecce Homo) is striking. According to popular tradition, the statue (the original of which is in the left transept at the entrance to the crypt, while that in the church proper is only a copy), irreverently called «Christ with a Toothache», was donated to the Cathedral by a sinner cured of a toothache and later converted.

On the north side of the Cathedral is the unfinished tower called the **Adlerturm** (Eagle's Tower). Sixty meters in height, it terminates with a Renaissance roof by the architect Hans Saphoy (1556-1578). The *Pummerin*, one of the world's largest bells, hangs in this tower: formed of 21,000 kg of bronze from Turkish cannons, the bell was re-cast after it was destroyed in 1945. An elevator takes us comfortably to the terrace of the tower, from which we can admire both the bell and the city panorama.

The exterior of the Stephansdom: the Capistrankanzel (Capistrano Pulpit).

Interior - In the interior of the church, with its richly-decorated nave and two aisles, all of equal size, elements in Gothic style unite with the Baroque to create a harmonious and utterly fascinating composition. The magnificent vault and the imposing columns are illuminated by the large windows, the original colored glass panes of which were destroyed in

View of the interior of the Stephansdom and the same subject in an engraving by Melchior Seltsam (1816).

1945. We will begin our tour of the Cathedral from the right aisle: in the **Herzogs-kapelle** (Ducal Chapel) or Chapel of Saint Elijah, a *statue of the Virgin Mary* dating to the 14th century merits attention. Under a canopy built between 1510 and 1515, illuminated by some hundred votive candles, is the miraculous image of the *Pötschen Madonna*, a painted icon from the Hungarian village of Pócs placed in the chapel in 1697. On a level with the transept is the entrance to the **Untere Sakristei**, an 18th-century Baroque addition with ceiling paintings by Altomonte.

The Pulpit by Anton Pilgram.

Facing page: the Four Fathers of the Church sculpted on the parapet of Pilgram's Pulpit. Below: Pilgram's self-portrait sculpted on the pulpit and that below the corbel of the organ.

The most valuable works in the Cathedral are found in the nave. The **Kanzel** (pulpit) by Anton Pilgram, against the third column on the right, is an incomparable masterpiece of Gothic art.

The figures of the *Four Fathers of the Church* (Augustine, Gregory, Jerome, Ambrose) representing the temperaments, and the richness of the detail on the pulpit as a whole make this work a harmonious jewel unique in its genre. The so-called *Fenstergucker* (Window-Gazer), is the self-portrait of Pilgram with which the artist «signed» his work: a masterpiece within a masterpiece.

Further along, together with a number of Baroque works, is the *Dienstbotenmadonna* (Madonna of the Servants) from the early 14th century. Legend has it that the work was donated by a noblewoman who had unjustly accused her chambermaid of theft.

At the beginning of the left aisle, closed off by a beautiful Baroque gate adorned with the coats-of-arms of the Savoias and the Liechtensteins, is the **Tirna- oder Kreuzkapelle** (Tirna Chapel or Chapel of the Cross) with the *tomb of Prince Eugene of Savoia*, the hero who repulsed the Turks from central Europe. Alongside is the beautiful *15th-century Gothic canopy* by Hans Prachatitz. Almost at the end of the aisle is another work by Pilgram: the 1513 organ base is a statue of the master craftsman himself (another «self-portrait») holding a square and compass. The organ has long since been moved. In the left transept is the **Crypt**, a simple room dating to 1752 and leading to the Catacombs, where since 1951 the mortal remains of the Archbishops of Vienna are entombed. In 1363, Rudolf IV ordered construction, in these subterranean vaults, of a crypt for the Dukes of Hapsburg. This was enlarged in 1754, during the reign of Maria Theresa, to house the copper urns containing the entrails of the members of the Hapsburg family; the em-

The *Dienstbotenmadonna (Madonna of the Servants)* and the *Wiener Neustädter Altarpiece.*

The High Altar by Johann Jakob Pock and Tobias Pock (1667).

balmed corpses instead rest in the Kapuzinergruft (Capuchin Crypt) and the hearts in the Augustinerkirche (Augustine Church).

The nave-and-two-aisle layout is repeated in the apsed choir. To the right, the **Apostelchor** (Apostles' Choir), with the *red marble tomb of Emperor Friedrich III,* is a fundamental work of the late Gothic funerary art of Niklas Gerhaert van Leyden, the most important Dutch sculptor of the time. Begun in 1469, it was unfinished at the time of both the artist's and the Emperor's deaths. Over the high altar at the end of the center choir is the Tobias Pock's Baroque altarpiece (1667) depicting the *Lapidation of Saint Stephan.*

The **Frauenchor** (Women's Gallery) closes off the left transept, with the Gothic *Wiener Neustädter Altar* of 1447, an altarpiece sculpted with scenes from the life of the Virgin Mary. It was brought here from the Wiener Neustadt in 1883 and installed in its present location in 1952. To the left is the *funeral monument to Rudolf IV and his wife Catherine of Bohemia* (ca. 1360/65).

STEPHANSPLATZ

Stephansplatz (Saint Stephan's Square) encircles the Cathedral; its present-day aspect dates to the 18th century and the square has gained in beauty since being included in the pedestrian zone.

Before leaving the square, we suggest entering the U-bahn station to visit the remains of the **Virgil-Kapelle** (Chapel of Saint Virgil). This is an authentic 13th-century crypt in the cemetery that until 1783 surrounded the cathedral; it was re-discovered during the excavation work for building the underground. At the chapel is also a collection of vases and other archaeological finds brought to light during excavation.

Facing the cathedral, to the left, a *Fiaker* stand awaits those whose program includes a romantic carriage-ride. The most noteworthy buildings on the square are the **Churhaus** (Curia) at No. 3, built between 1738 and 1740, the **Domherren-Hof** (Priest's Lodge) at No. 5 and the **Dom- und Diözesanmuseum** (Cathedral and Diocesan Museum) at No. 6. In the Treasury and in five other rooms, this museum displays precious paintings, sculptures and other examples of sacred art from the early Middle Ages through the Baroque periods. Of particular interest is the portrait of Duke Rudolf IV: presumably painted in about 1360 in the court workshop of Prague, it depicts one of the most important of the Cathedral's patrons; it is believed to be the earliest portrait of the Duke and shows him three-quarters profile, a departure from the traditional full-profile figure. Also of great importance are the altarpiece from Antwerp, sculpted in about 1450, and the Ober-St. Veit altarpiece, the Crucifixion of which is considered to be the most important German pictorial work of the early 16th century. It is by Dürer's pupil Hans Schäufelein.

Almost across from the «Steffl», with its entrance at No. 7 of nearby Singerstrasse, we find the **Kirche und Schatzkammer des Deutschen Ordens** (Church and Treasury of the Teutonic Order). Consecrated in 1375, the church is one of the few Gothic buildings in which the transformations in Baroque style, with its characteristic oval elements, create a harmonious Gothic-Baroque composition.

The noteworthy *Flügelaltar* (Triptych), a 16th-century Dutch work, was in Danzig's Marienkirche until 1864. The **Schatzkammer** is also worth a visit: here are exhibited precious tableware and household furnishings from the 17th and 18th centuries as well as signs, coins, ceremonial costumes and arms.

The Erlach Madonna (ca. 1325), Saint Rochus (ca. 1500) and the «Lament of Christ» in the Cathedral and Diocesan Museum.

View of the Graben with the Plague Column. Below: On the Graben. *Engraving by Carl Schütz (1782).*

GRABEN

The Graben, together with the Kärntnerstrasse and the Kohlmarkt, is the elegant shopping district of Vienna, a street for first-class purchases, a classical site for rendez-vous and meetings.

In the pedestrian area, the Graben strikes us due to its unusual form: a large, elongated square. About 300 meters in length and over 30 wide, the square lies over the moat of the ancient Roman castrum, which was filled in during the late 12th century and transformed into a wide street. At the time, of Maria Theresa it became the famous meeting-place for the Vienna that counted and the no less famous center of high-class prostitution («Grabennymphen»). At the center of the square rises the Baroque **Pestsäule** (Plague Column) which was commissioned by Emperor Leopold I in thanks for the end of the Plague of 1679 and erected by Johann Bernard Fischer von Erlach and Ludovico Ottavio Burnacini with the collaboration of other important artists of the time.

The two ends of the Graben are adorned by two 19th-century fountains. Also of note are a number of buildings from the same century, such as the Biedermeier-style **Erste Österreichische Sparkasse** (First Austrian Savings Bank) at No. 21 and the Jugendstil buildings at Nos.

The Baroque Peterskirche (Saint Peter's Church). Below: the Peterskirche as depicted in an engraving by Carl Schütz (1779).

10, 14-15 and 16. The facade of the latter is decorated with floral motifs in colored majolica. To the right of the Graben as we come from the Cathedral is the Petersplatz on which the **Peterskirche** (Saint Peter's Church) is located. The Baroque church was built, with the collaboration of J. Lukas von Hildebrandt, in 1702-1715 on the site of an ancient church which according to legend was built by order of Charlemagne. The **interior**, with frescoes and ochre and gold stuccowork, is the work of the most famous Baroque artists including M. Altomonte, L.

Mattielli, M. Steindl, S. Bussi and A. Camesina. The *fresco of the Dome* is a masterpiece by J. M. Rottmayr.

AM HOF

The beautiful, ancient and elegant Naglergasse, also pedestrianized, leads from the Graben to the medieval city center and to the large square called Am Hof: trapezoidal in form, center of city political life through the centuries, it is still today one of the city's most significant sites. It was here that in the 12th century the Babenbergs built their Residence; in the past, tournaments and festivals were organized in this square delimited by beautiful homes and a church. At the center rises the **Mariensäule** (Column of Our Lady), promised to the Madonna by Emperor Ferdinand III in his prayers during the war against the Swedes and erected between 1664 and 1667 in place of a 1647 column. The triumphant Mary Immaculate tramples the serpent of the Apocalypse, while on the base

Above: Pope Pius VI blessing the faithful from the balcony on the façade in 1782 (engraving by Carl Schütz).
The Kirche «Am Hof», or Church of the Nine Choirs of Angels.

*The Mariensäule
(Column of Our Lady)
of «Am Hof».*

*The Zeughaus, once the city
arsenal.*

Palais Daun-Kinsky on the Freyung, facing the Schottenkirche (Scottish Church).

armed angels battle four dragons, symbols of the four great scourges of mankind: war, famine, plague and heresy.

The **Kirche «Am Hof»** , or Church of the Nine Choirs of Angels, built by the Carmelite friars in about 1400, was restored in 1607-1610 in Baroque style in the interior following a fire. The sumptuous facade of 1662, a beautiful example of early Baroque, was redesigned by the Italian architect C. A. Carlone. The walls, side chapels and dome in the **interior**, a Gothic structure with two aisles and a nave, are decorated with frescoes and stucco-work. On the high altar is a large altarpiece by J. G. Däringer, *Maria and the Choir of Angels.* In 1782, Pope Pius VI blessed the Viennese from the balcony of the facade, and on 6 August 1806 the renunciation of Emperor Franz II to the crown of the Holy Roman Empire was proclaimed from the same balcony. This secular political unit thus came to an end under pressure from Napoleon's forces.

It was in the **Palais Collalto**, at No. 13 next door to the church, that in 1762 Wolfgang Amadeus Mozart held his first concert in Vienna. In a corner of the square, in what was formerly the **Bürgerliches Zeughaus** (City Arsenal), a 16th-century building with statues by Lorenzo Mattielli on the facade, are the headquarters of the Fire Brigade.

In one of the narrow old streets behind the «Am Hof» church, at No. 2 of the Schulhof, is the **Uhrenmuseum** (Clock Museum): it is one of the most interesting of its kind and a gem among the city's museums. The three floors of the small, old building exhibit over 3000 time-pieces, some of which are true masterpieces of mechanics. Of note for their sheer richness are those with inlays in ivory, enamel, silver and precious stones; and for its oddity a time-piece of rural origin with a pendulum in the form of a cow's tail. From the astronomical clock, the hands of which take 20,904 years to make one complete revolution, to the most precious of pocket watches: there is something for everyone.

FREYUNG

A short street links the «Am Hof» square and the «Freyung», another suggestive square of old Vienna. Of irregular form and encircled by beautiful palaces and the Scottish Church, its name (from frei, *«free») dates back to the Middle Ages, when the Scottish Convent offered sanctuary to the persecuted; the poor reputation that accompanied the area for centuries may also date to the same period. The square also offers other artistic attractions: at No. 3 is found the **Palais Harrach**, built in 1690 from a plan by Domenico Martinelli; at No. 4 the **Palais Daun-Kinsky**, one of the most beautiful Baroque buildings in Vienna, built in the years 1713-1716 by J. Lukas von Hildebrandt, with a great staircase of particular interest in the interior; No. 7 is called **«Schubladkastenhaus»** (Chest of Drawers House), a strange name for the 16th-century Priory of the Scottish Convent - but as to form it does resemble a dresser. In the square is also found the **Austria-Brunnen** (Austria Fountain) designed by Ludwig Schwanthaler; this symbolic representation of Austria and the four great rivers of the Hapsburg Empire (Po, Vistula, Elbe and Danube) was built in 1846.*

Schottenkirche - The origins of the Scottish Church date back to the 12th century, to when Duke Heinrich Jasomirgott, the first of the Babenbergs to reside in Vienna, called in the Irish Benedictine monks from Ratisbona and donated large sums to their order. The monks, who during the Middle Ages were always erroneously called «Schotten» (Scotch), built the first Romanesque church. It was damaged many times over the following centuries by fires and collapses; it was rebuilt in Gothic style following the earthquake of 1443. The Gothic altar had 24 important paintings by Scottish masters, 19 of which are on display in the convent gallery. Today's Baroque aspect dates to the years 1643-1648, and is the work of the Italian ar-

The Benedictine church known as the Schottenkirche or Scottish Church, on the Freyung. Facing page: the Austria-Brunnen. Below: a portrait of the writer Peter Altenberg at the Café Central.

chitects Andrea Felice d'Allio and Silvestro Carlone; the latest alterations date to the 19th century. Two heavy, low towers embellish the linear facade. In the **interior** are the two highly valuable Baroque side altars, the *Deckengemälde* (ceiling paintings) of the nave, executed by Julius Schmid in 1887-1889, and the *high altar*, work of H. Ferstel (1883). To the left is the entrance to the *crypt,* the burial place of Duke Heinrich II Jasomirgott. On the left side altar stands the most ancient statue of the Virgin Mary in all Vienna, dating to about 1250; it is said that the statue saved the city from the Swedish seige near the end of the Thirty Years' War.

Freyung-Passage - Between the Freyung and the Herrengasse is a hidden passage that must be considered a true «jewel» . In the so-called Palais Ferstel, which in the mid-19th century was the headquarters of the Austro-Hungarian Bank, the passage had fallen into decay and only recently, following massive restoration work, has it regained its ancient splendor. Passages, courtyards, marble staircases of varied hues covered by glass vaults, and a small, gracious square with the **Brunnen der Donaunymphen** (Fountain of the Danube Water-Sprites) are the ideal setting for a pleasant shopping trip to the modern, elegant shops. The completely restored Café Central, a meeting-place of intellectuals and writers during the last decades of the Monarchy, invites you to stop for coffee and a sweet.

Amalienburg, the
Leopoldinischer
Trakt • 41

«In der Burg»
• 40, 41

State Apartments • 38, 39

Heldenplatz • 44

The Volksgarten
• 46, 47

The Spanish
Riding School
• 50, 51

Neue Burg, the
Neue Hofburg
Museums • 44/ 47

The Imperial Ch
• 42, 43

The Hofburg • 37/51

The Alte
Burg • 42/44

34

The Michaelertrakt • 38

...haelerplatz • 36

Michaelerplatz - **Hofburg** - Michaelertrakt - **Kaiserappartements** (State Apartments) - **«In der Burg»** - Amalienburg - Leopoldinischer Trakt - Reichskanzleitrakt - Alte Burg - Burgkapelle (Imperial Chapel) - **Weltliche und Geistliche Schatzkammer** (Sacred and Secular Treasuries) - Heldenplatz - Neue Burg - Neue Hofburg Museums - Hofburg Gardens - Stallburg - Josefsplatz - Nationalbibliothek (National Library) - **Spanische Hofreitschule** (Spanish Riding School) - Augustinerkirche (Augustine Church) - Albertina.

The Imperial Chancery • 42

The Imperial Treasuries • 43, 44

The Stallburg • 48

Josefsplatz, the National Library • 48/ 50

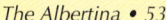

The Albertina • 53

The Augustinerkirche • 52

MICHAELERPLATZ

This beautiful, almost triangular square is the starting point for those who wish to visit «Imperial» Vienna. The statues and the fountains of the Michaelertrakt are but the prelude to the Imperial Residence, which was the hub of an empire with 50 million subjects.
This square, with its many important monuments, merits much more than a passing glance.

The **Michaelerkirche** (Saint Michael's Church) attracts attention immediately. This late Romanesque edifice, raised during the first half of the 13th century, was enlarged and transformed over the centuries that followed in the Gothic, Baroque and classicized styles. The Neo-Classical facade by E. Koch (1793) is simple and unadorned; it is preceded by the Baroque porch by A. Beduzzi, dating to 1724-1725, topped by the sculptural group of the *Archangel Michael* by L. Mattielli. The soaring bell-tower (1598), with its many pinnacles, stands guard over the church. The interior has a nave and two aisles with a transept and choir; above the high altar (1781), Vienna's last Baroque work, is a 16th-century *Byzantine icon* from Crete. The mortal remains of the poet Pietro Metastasio repose in the left transept; Karl Georg Mervill is the author of the main choir with the famous *Fall of the Angels.*
Across from the church rises the sober and again unadorned facade of the Loos Haus, in evident contrast with the richness of the architecture of the Imperial Palace. The **Loos Haus** takes its name from Adolf Loos, the important exponent of the Viennese Jugendstil who built it in 1910. Its simplicity would represent a protest against what was called the «Ring Style» with its monumental forms and excessive ornamentation. The Emperor Franz Joseph, who could not stand the sight of this bare building across from his windows, was outraged by its construction. The **Kohlmarkt**, the animated business street that leads to the Graben, opens off Michaelerplatz. You will find the famous Konditorei Demel, a classic among Viennese gastronomical addresses, at No. 11 in the Kohlmarkt.

Michaelerkirche
(Saint Michael's Church).

View of the interior.

Monumental entrance to the Hofburg in the Michaelertrakt (Saint Michael's Wing). Below: the two fountains at the ends of the building.

HOFBURG

For more than six centuries the Hofburg was the Residence of the Hapsburgs, who governed there first as Emperors of the Holy Roman Empire and from 1806 onwards as Emperors of Austria. Frequent additions and transformations have made of it a complex embracing 18 buildings, 19 courtyards, 54 staircases and 2600 rooms. The Hofburg has no intrinsic architectural unity; it is rather the legacy of a centuries-long history in which each epoch has left its mark: thus in a certain sense the complex represents a historical/artistic compendium of the Hapsburg monarchy. In these halls, stipulations of treaties of state and declarations of war were interspersed with merry balls; political intrigues and love stories, revolutions and fires and six sieges made of the Hofburg for many centuries the main theatre of Austrian history. And still today, the Hofburg carries on an important function in the political life of the country: it is home to the offices of the federal President and an important international meeting center.

The old Burgtheater on the Michaelerplatz, in a water-color by Carl Schütz (ca. 1783).

Michaelertrakt (Saint Michael's Wing) - Built between 1883 and 1893 where the Burgtheater once stood, from a partly-modified draft plan by the great architect Joseph Emanuel Fischer von Erlach, the Michaelertrakt became the main entrance to the Hofburg. Excavations in front of the entrance have revealed remains from Roman times, the Middle Ages, and the 18th century. A circular hall surmounted by a great dome leads from the Michaelerplatz to the inner courtyard, called «**In der Burg**». The facade is adorned with two fountains celebrating the power of the Hapsburgs over land and sea. That on the right represents the *Dominion of Austria on Land* (1897), that on the left the *Dominion of Austria on the Sea* (1895).
The entrance to the State Apartments is to the left of the Michaelertor as we come from the Michaelerplatz.

Kaiserappartements - Those of the State Apartments open to the public (guided visits) are all located in the wing housing the Reichskanzlei (Imperial Chancery) and the Amalienburg. An important visit this, one not to be missed, since wandering through the Emperor's rooms is certainly not something one can do every day. And it is a visit that will give us an idea of the difference between the simple lifestyle of Emperor Franz Joseph and that of his royal consort Elizabeth, who took care of her perfect body to the extreme with baths, beauty masks and physical exercise. We can admire the refined Rococo furnishings or the exquisite Empire style (Louis XV) furniture and the splendid chandeliers in Bohemian crystal in the beautiful rooms that hosted Czar Alexander I during the Congress of Vienna (1815); further along is the banquet room with its table laid for dinner.

The Kaiserappartements (Imperial Apartments): the bedroom of Emperor Franz Joseph; below: the boudoir of Empress Elizabeth.

Our tour begins with the **Apartment of Archduke Stephan**, four rooms with valuable *Brussels tapestries* dating to the 17th century. Next is the **Apartment of Franz Joseph**, which includes among other attractions the Audience Chamber, with mural paintings by Peter Krafft, and the Conference Hall. The **Apartment of the Empress Elizabeth** is made up of six rooms; of particular interest are the bedroom and the bath (or dressing room), and the *statue of Elisa Bonaparte* by Antonio Canova (1817). The **Apartment of Alexander** contains 6 rooms featuring precious 18th-century Parisian wall-coverings; the **State Banqueting Hall** concludes the series of rooms open to the public. On one side of the entrance hall is the entrance to the **Hofsilber- und Tafelkammer** (Room of Tableware and Silver),

The Kaiserappartements (Imperial Apartments):
the Imperial Banqueting Hall.

where a precious *collection of Chinese and Japanese porcelain* from the 18th century, a *Sèvres dinner service*, a vermilion dinner service for 140, a 33-meter long 19th-century bronze centerpiece and other court tableware are displayed.

«In der Burg» - As we exit the Michaelertrakt rotunda we come to this broad inner yard built in 1545 for Archduke Maximilian, as a tournament ground. If the Schweizerhof can be said to represent the Gothic Hofburg and the Heldenplatz to embody the spirit of the 19th century, in the «In der Burg» square the Baroque has left clear and lasting marks. It was originally used for celebrations and tournaments (worth mention, above all, the famous ballet of horses given on the occasion of the wedding of Leopold I to Margherita of Spain in

The courtyard known as «In der Burg» with the Leopoldinischertrakt (Leopoldine Wing) on the left, and the Amalienburg. Facing, the monument to Emperor Franz I.

1666), but it was also the theatre of dramatic events such as the execution of officials and soldiers during the Turkish Wars. At the center of the yard is the *monument to Emperor Franz I*, who died in 1835. The sumptuous Schweizertor (Swiss Portal) leads in to the Schweizerhof.

Amalienburg - This wing of the castle, commissioned by the Emperor Rudolf II, was erected between 1575 and 1611. The interior was completely renovated during the reign of Maria Theresa. Of note the **Turm** (Tower) added by Nikolaus Pacassi in 1764; the *lunar clock* that marks the phases of the moon is the work of Tycho de Brahes, well-known astronomer at the court of Rudolf II. The name of the building derives from that of the Empress Amalia, the widow of Joseph I, who lived here from 1711 until her death in 1742.

Leopoldinischer Trakt (Leopoldine Wing) - Begun by Emperor Ferdinand I in 1547, construction of this wing of the Hofburg, added to link the Schweizerhof and the Amalienburg, was continued during the years from 1660 through 1667 by Emperor Leopold I; destroyed by the fire of 1668, the wing was finally lived in by the Emperor in 1681. Baroque additions were introduced in the entire Imperial Residence following Austria's victory over the Turks. Empress Maria Theresa and her husband Franz Stephan of Lorraine lived in this part of the palace, which is still furnished with the Empress' luxurious furniture. Since 1946, the wing has been the official residence of the federal President, whose attendance is signalled by the flying of the flag.

The Reichskanzleitrakt (Imperial Chancery).

Reichskanzleitrakt (Imperial Chancery) - J. Lukas von Hildebrandt and Joseph Emanuel Fischer von Erlach began construction of this north wing of the Imperial Residence in 1723; it was completed in 1730. The *Labors of Hercules* that decorate the main entrance are the work of Lorenzo Mattielli. The wing was the seat of government of the Holy Roman Empire until 1806.

Alte Burg - This fortified building, mentioned for the first time on 14 February 1279 in a document by King Rudolf I Hapsburg, was probably begun some years earlier (1275) by order of King Ottakar II of Bohemia. Of the original square-based construction with four massive corner keeps there remains only the **Schweizerhof** (Swiss Courtyard), which however underwent major transformation in the 16th century and so lost its medieval look. The name derives from the Swiss Guard, which garrisoned the castle during the time of Maria Theresa.

The Renaissance Schweizertor (Swiss Portal).

The **Schweizertor** (Swiss Portal) is a sumptuous brick-colored Renaissance portal with gold inscriptions. It was erected in 1552 on the spot where the drawbridge stood in the 13th century.

The Schweizerhof gives access to the **Burgkapelle** (Imperial Chapel). Perhaps the oldest part of the Hofburg, the construction dates to the years 1447-1449, when it was built by order of Friedrich III in place of an earlier chapel built for Duke Albrecht I (1296). Of considerable value are the late Gothic wooden sculptures, displayed on stands under canopies, representing the 14 Protector Saints and presumably made in the style of Niklas Gerhaert van Leyden, who also sculpted the funerary monument to Emperor Friedrich III, in the Stephansdom.

The Schatzkammer (Imperial Treasuries): the crown of the Holy Roman Empire and the cloak of Emperor Franz I.

On the tabernacle of the high altar is a small wooden crucifix. It seems that the Emperor Ferdinand II, sorely contrasted by the Protestant orders of Lower Austria in their fight for freedom of religion, heard Christ whisper from this crucifix: «Ferdinand, I shall not abandon you!» Since that time a copy of this cross is found in every Hapsburg chapel. It is in this chapel that the Wiener Sängerknaben (Vienna Boys' Choir) sings during the Sunday morning Mass.

From the Schweizerhof we go on to one of the most famous and most valuable collections in the world: the **Weltliche und Geistliche Schatzkammer** (Sacred and Profane Treasuries), where hundreds of objects of inestimable value bear witness to the long and complex history of the Holy Roman Empire and its close ties with the Catholic Church.

Twenty-one rooms are host to this collection of precious objects in gold, silver and gems as well as exquisite embroideries and fabrics: the 10th-century *Imperial crown*, the 12th-century *Imperial globe*, the *silver sceptre*, the 12th-century Chinese silk *incoronation cloak* sewn in Palermo for King Roger II, the *Hapsburg Imperial crown* («Hauskrone») dating to 1602, the *baptismal pitcher and bowl* used for Imperial family christenings, and the *silver cradle*, weighing a good 280 kilograms, given by the City of Paris to Napoleon I for his son, the King of

The sweeping Heldenplatz, with the Neue Burg.
Below: the Äusseres Burgtor, the external gate opening onto the Ring.

Rome. A special place is reserved for the «Treasure of the Knights of the Golden Fleece», or the «Burgundian Inheritance», which with the wedding of Maximilian I to Mary of Burgundy became a Hapsburg possession; the Hapsburgs thus also inherited the title of «Dukes of Burgundy». Outstanding among the many highly valuable items in the collection is a masterpiece of medieval art, 15th century *Burgundian vestments*. The Sacred Treasury conserves liturgical ornaments and vestments and relics used and collected at Court. One of the most valuable pieces is the *reproduction of the «Am Hof» Mariensäule*, created in 1670-1680 by the goldsmith Philipp Kösel of Augsburg, who set in it over 3700 precious and semi-precious stones.

Heldenplatz - From the «In der Burg» square, through a passage running under the Leopoldine Wing, we come to the vast Heldenplatz (Heroes' Square), once used for military reviews of the Imperial Army. The square is dominated by two great *equestrian statues*, one of *Grand Duke Karl* and the other of *Prince Eugene of Savoia*. The hemicycle of the Neue

Burg opens at the end of the square; facing the Leopoldine Wing is the Äusseres Burgtor, and on its the right the square borders on the Volksgarten.

Neue Burg - This grandiose palace, completed in 1913, is the last construction bearing witness to Hapsburg

power. It was originally the first portion of a project by G. Semper for construction of a colossal «Imperial Forum» ; the defeat of the Austro-Hungarian monarchy in 1918 put an end to this dream of glory. The part that links up to Leopoldine Wing includes a gigantic hall of over 1000 square meters area, designed for court festivities and today used as a meeting hall. The building houses a number of museums and a portion of the National Library.

The Neue Hofburg Museums - We have already spoken of some of the Hofburg museums; there follows an introduction to the others.

Ephesos-Museum - In the first years of the 20th century and again after the end of World War II, Austrian archaeologists were involved in excavations in Asia Minor and in particular in Ephesus in Turkey.
The finds from this region are displayed in this museum according to the most up-to-date exhibit criteria.
Worthy of attention here are the *colossal frieze* from the 2nd century AD, over 70 meters in length, commemorating the victory of Lucius Verus and Marcus Aurelius over the Parthians in 165 AD; and the *octagonal tomb* of a young woman and a part of the *sacrificial altar* of the great Temple of Artemides. The same entrance ticket also permits us to visit the **Waffensammlung** (Weapons Collection) containing historic armor and ceremonial weapons, and the **Sammlung alter Musikinstrumente** (Collection of Ancient Musical Instruments) with its Renaissance instruments, harpsichords, pianos and many others, including the instruments used by the most illustrious of Austrian musicians (Brahms, Haydn, Schubert, Beethoven).
The **Museum für Völkerkunde** (Ethnological Museum) houses objects from all parts of the world.
Among these, on the ground floor, are the famous bronze statues from the Kingdom of

Ancient armor from the Weapons Collection at the Neue Hofburg.

The Theseus-Tempel (Temple of Theseus) and the fountain memorial to Empress Elizabeth, in the Volksgarten.

Benin (an African kingdom the golden age of which dates from the 12th to the 18th centuries) and the celebrated *crown of feathers* and the *shield* given by the Aztec Emperor Montezuma to Fernando Cortez as a token of friendship. The first-floor exhibits include, among other things, handcrafted articles from Brazil, New Guinea and Australia.

Hofburg Gardens - Our visit to the Hofburg is certainly an extenuating one: halls, staircases, courtyards and museums; a place to rest a while, suspending for a moment our walk, is a welcome relief. We therefore suggest a pause, and the Hofburg complex embraces not one but two parks that admirably serve the purpose: the **Volksgarten** (Public Garden) and the **Burggarten** (Castle Garden). The former is next to the

Heldenplatz, in the direction of the Burgtheater; the other lies behind the Neue Burg. These two green oases, replete with fountains and statues, offer us the opportunity to relax in a natural setting of massive horse-chestnut trees and rose-beds. In the Volksgarten we find the monument to Empress Elizabeth («Sissy»), where young couples habitually meet. In the Burggarten, instead, don't forget to stop at the *Mozart Memorial*, or to stroll along the shores of the

The monuments to Emperor Franz Joseph, Goethe, and Mozart, in the Burggarten.

lake, or to see the monument to Emperor Franz Joseph and the Jugendstil *palm greenhouse*.
Different epochs and styles overlay each other in the Hofburg complex, and while the effect as a whole is harmonious, it demands of the visitor his undivided attention. Visiting the Hofburg is tantamount to making a journey through the cen-

47

turies of Hapsburg dominion. Upon concluding our visit, we suggest returning through the «In der Burg» square and the Michaelertor to the Michaelerplatz, on the right of which we find still another interesting wing of the Hofburg.

The inner courtyard of the Stallburg (Imperial Stables). Below: Josefsplatz with the Nationalbibliothek (National Library) building and the equestrian monument to Joseph II.

Stallburg (Imperial Stables) - The inner courtyard is perhaps the most beautiful Renaissance work in all of Vienna. Built between 1558 and 1565 by Ferdinand I for his son Maximilian, it was originally separated from the Hofburg and consisted of a large square courtyard with colonnaded sides. It was later transformed to provide stables for the Emperor's horses, and is today the stable of the Spanish Riding School. The Stallburg also hosts the Lipizzaner Museum (Museum of the Lipizzaner Horse), which is well worth a visit.

Josefsplatz - In this square, one of the most beautiful and harmonious in all Vienna, the 18th century has without doubt left works of high artistic and architectural value. Surrounded

by splendid buildings, the square was until 1565 the riding-ground of the Spanish Riding School; only under Emperor Joseph II did it take on its present-day look. At the center of the square the *equestrian statue*, sculpted in 1795-1807 in a style recalling antiquity by Franz Anton Zauner, celebrates Joseph II.

Looking toward the National Library which runs down one entire side of the square, we see on the right the **Redoutensäle** (Redoute Rooms), dating to 1767 and formerly used as ballrooms and for theatrical events. On the left

Josefsplatz: Palais Pallavicini. Below: the «Hofbibliothek», or Court Library, in an engraving by Carl Schütz (1780).

is a wing of the Augustine convent, and across from the Library are the beautiful **Palais Pallavicini** (1784) and **Palais Palffy** (1575).

Nationalbibliothek - The building that houses the National Library is again linked to the names of the two greatest architects of the Baroque, Fischer von Erlach father and son; it was the latter who completed the building in 1735. The *Prunksaal* (Hall of Honor) is decorated with frescoes by Daniel Gran. The library owns about 7 million items, 2,500,000 of which

are books, 300,000 manuscripts and incunabula, 183,000 papyri, 1,300,000 items in the theatrical collection and 1,600,000 between the portrait collection and the iconographic archives. The rarest and most valuable specimens are on exhibit in the rooms open to the public.

Spanische Hofreitschule - White horses and proud riders in a setting of unequalled beauty and elegance: this is the Spanish Riding School. It has existed for over 400 years and is the greatest attraction in the Hofburg and indeed in all Vienna. In order to attend the performances you must make reservations many months in advance, but it is instead much easier to see the Lipizzaner horses at their morning training sessions, held every day except Sunday and Monday from February through June and from September through December. The queue to see this show, truly unique in the world, is worth every minute: the exercises performed with apparent ease and naturalness require years of training and a perfect concord between horse and rider that is extremely difficult to achieve. The Spanish Riding School was created in 1572 for military purposes. Originally, the horses were all Spanish and were destined for front-line combat alongside the

The Prunksaal, the gala hall of the National Library.
Below: an acrobatic performance by the Spanische Hofreitschule (Spanish Riding School).

The Lipizzaner horses of the Spanish Riding School are one of Vienna's major attractions.

regular cavalry. Today, the Lipizzaner horses are raised at the Piber Castle, near Graz. The school is housed in the **Winterreitschule** (Winter Riding School) built between 1729 and 1735 under the direction of J. E. Fischer von Erlach. The hub of the building is the hall, 55 meters in length, where the horses train and perform. This all-white hall is flooded with light and encircled by 46 columns that support the gallery. At the time of the Congress of Vienna, sensational celebrations were held here: for example, that on 2 October 1814, attended by 10,000 guests. The hall has also been the theatre of political events, such as the assembly of the citizenry during the 1848 Revolution. The Summer Riding School is located at the rear of the building.

From the Josefsplatz, we continue down the Augustinerstrasse to the last two stops on our itinerary: the Augustine Church and the Albertina.

The marriage of Emperor Franz Joseph and Elizabeth in the Augustinerkirche (Augustinian Church), in a lithograph by Vinzenz Katzler (1854).

Augustinerkirche - The Court parish church, where Imperial weddings were held, was built in the 14th century in Gothic style. The interior was later remodelled in the Baroque style, but in 1784-1785 was again «Gothicized» .

Interior - The Augustinerkirche is a high, narrow church with two aisles and a nave, all very simple in style. At the beginning of the right aisle we see the *funerary monument to Archduchess Maria Christina* (favorite daughter of Maria Theresa) who died in 1798. It is a Neo-Classical work by Antonio Canova dating to 1798-1805. On the right, alongside the choir, is the two-aisled 14th-century **St. Georgskapelle** (Saint George's Chapel). The Augustine Church, like others in Vienna, is a Hapsburg burial place. A niche in the Chapel houses the **Herzgruft**, where 54 silver urns each containing the heart of a member of the Imperial family are kept. The «oldest» heart is that of Ferdinand II (1578-1637), while the latest arrival is that of Archduke Franz Karl (1802-1878), father of Emperor Franz Joseph.

Augustinerkirche: the interior of the church and the funerary monument of Archduchess Maria Christina.

Albertina - The name derives from that of its founder, Duke Albert of Sachen-Teschen. The palace, enlarged in the years 1801-1804, houses one of the world's largest graphics collections (**Graphische Sammlung**), with about 40,000 drawings and more than one million prints. Among other items, the collection includes works by Leonardo da Vinci, Raphael, Rubens, Rembrandt, Cranach, Brueghel and Dürer as well as by the modern artists Picasso, Matisse and Chagall. Exhibits of certain sections of the collections open to the public are held periodically.

A staircase beginning at the museum entrance leads up to the panoramic terrace on which we find the *equestrian statue of Arch-duke Albrecht*; from here, on the right, another flight of stairs leads down to the Burggarten.

Albertina: the Danube fountain at the Albrechtsrampe; «The Hare» by Albrecht Dürer.

The Albertina with the statue of Arch-duke Albrecht.

Maria am Gestade
• 63/65

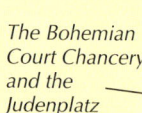

Hoher Markt
• 61, 62

The Alte Universit
• 61

Maria am
Gestade

Altes
Rathaus
ghaus

The Bohemian
Court Chancery
and the
Judenplatz
• 63

Böhmische
Hofkanzlei

**irche
m Hof"**

Salvatorgasse

Aurel

Marc

Tuchlauben

Brandstätte

Peters-
kirche

Graben

Dom-und
Diözesan
mus.

The Altes Rathaus • 62, 63

k.

Brauerstr

Spiegelgasse

Steph

Kärntner Straße

Kärtnerstrasse • 57

Stallburg

Pal.
Pallavicini

Pal.
Lobkowitz

Kapuziner-
kirche

ustinerk.

Augustinerstr.

Tegetthoffstr.

Pal. des
Prinzen Eugen

Johann

Him

Straße

Albertina

EN

Albertina-
platz

Walfis

The Kaisergruft • 57, 58

gasse

Staatsoper

Albertina-
passage

ring

Opern-
passage

The Hotel Sacher • 56

The Staatsoper • 56

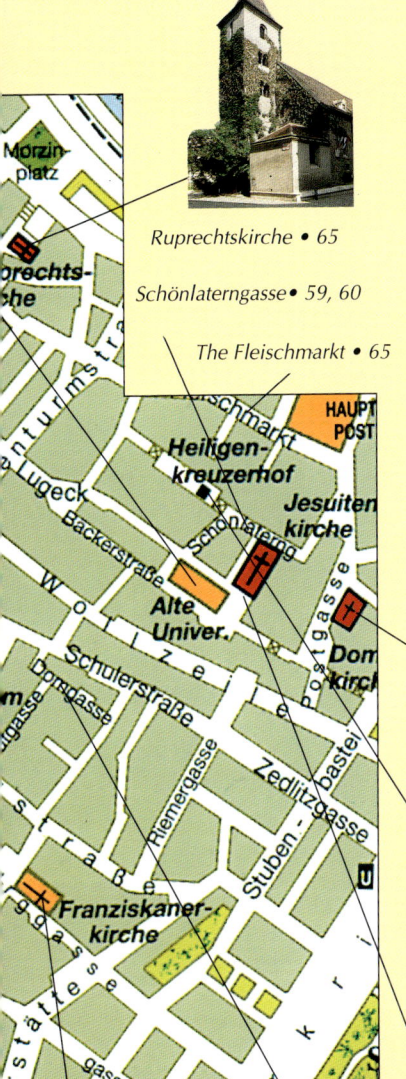

ITINERARY III

Staatsoper - Hotel Sacher - **Kärntnerstrasse** - **Kaisergruft** (Imperial Crypt) - Stadtpalais des Prinzen Eugen (Winter Palace of Prince Eugene) - Franziskanerkirche (Franciscan Church) - Figarohaus (House of Figaro) - Dominikanerkirche (Dominican Church) - Schönlaterngasse - Heiligenkreuzerhof - Bernhardskapelle (Chapel of Saint Bernard) - Jesuitenkirche (Jesuit Church) - Akademie der Wissenschaften (Academy of Sciences) - Alte Universität - **Hoher Markt** - **Altes Rathaus** - Böhmische Hofkanzlei - Judenplatz - **Maria am Gestade** (Church of Saint Mary on the Bank) - Fleischmarkt - **Ruprectskirche** (Church of Saint Ruprecht).

Ruprechtskirche • 65

Schönlaterngasse • 59, 60

The Fleischmarkt • 65

The Dominikanerkirche • 59

The Heiligenkreuzerhof and the Bernhardskapelle • 60, 61

The Jesuit Church, The Academy of Sciences • 60, 61

Figarohaus • 59

The Franziskanerkirche • 58

The Winter Palace of Prince Eugene • 58

55

STAATSOPER

Haydn, Mozart, Beethoven, Schubert, Strauss: these few names suffice to suggest the importance of Vienna in the history of world music. With the Scala of Milan and the Metropolitan of New York, the Vienna State Opera House is one of the most famous theaters in the world; here are held magnificent theatrical events as well as the famous Opera Ball that recreates for spectator the ancient splendor of the Imperial capital.

Construction work on the Staatsoper, completed in 1869, was the subject of violent debate which eventually caused the deaths of the architects who had designed it, E. van der Null and A. von Siccardsburg: one committed suicide and the other died of a heart attack two months later. Neither was able to attend the inaugural performance of Mozart's *Don Giovanni* in 1869.

In 1945, the Opera was almost completely destroyed by bombing. It was rebuilt after the war to incorporate the most advanced technology of the time; today's auditorium boasts a seating capacity of 2209.

Guided tours give us an idea of the interior, with the splendid Grand Staircase with its *statues of the nine Muses* by Joseph Grasser, the beautiful frescoed lunettes of the foyer, and the boxes by Moritz von Schwind, miraculously intact despite the damage caused by the war. Outside, to the sides of the Opera building, are two graceful fountains. Behind the imposing theater is another well-known attraction of Vienna (especially for those with a sweet tooth): the **Hotel Sacher**. Always a venue for «the Vienna that counts» , it was also theatre of political intrigues, secret meetings and love stories of European-scale resonance. The name naturally evokes the famous *Sachertorte*, a specialty of Viennese cuisine.

The nineteenth-century neo-Renaissance Staatsoper building.
Above: W. A. Mozart portrayed in an engraving by Johann Neidl.

The Haashaus on the Stephansplatz.

KÄRTNERSTRASSE

This wide street linking the Ring, with Saint Stephan's Square is part, together with the Graben, of the pedestrian area and may be considered the elegant «promenade» of Vienna. The benches under the horse chestnut trees beckon us, promising a relaxing pause and, in summer, the tables of the many cafés and restaurants are very pleasant stopping and meeting places. Young musicians offer a romantic parenthesis for those who stroll down this street at leisure. Lining the route are luxury boutiques and famous cafés (like the «Sirk», at No. 53, across from the Opera), a tradition that has become a part of Viennese culture. On the right in the first stretch is the **Malteserkirche**, a small Gothic church, dating perhaps to the 14th century, with a Neo-Classical facade, containing memorabilia of the medieval Order of the Knights of Malta.

A short street at about the level of this church leads to the *Neuer Markt.* At the point in which the Kärtnerstrasse runs into Saint Stephan's Square there stands the trunk of an old tree, called the **«Stock im Eisen»**, in which every craftsman who left the city in olden times was wont to plant a nail to ensure that he would return. Facing the Stephansdom is the **Haashaus**, with its surprising asymmetrical facade. This building is the work of the famous Austrian architect Hans Hollein, who completed it in 1990.

KAISERGRUFT

The **Neuer Markt** (New Market) Square is home to the **Kapuzinerkirche** (Capuchin Church), a small Baroque building erected in the years from 1622 to 1632 and selected by the Hapsburgs for celebrating the funeral cere-

The Kapuzinerkirche (Capuchin Church). Below: the funerary monument to Maria Theresa and her husband in the Kaisergruft (Imperial Founders Crypt).

monies for members of the Imperial family. To the side of the facade we note a closed portal, behind which - if we have it opened - a long passage and a narrow staircase lead to the Kaisergruft, the imposing Hapsburg Crypt, where since 1633 all the members of the family, including 12 Emperors and 16 Empresses, have been entombed. Through these ten unadorned rooms there runs before the visitor's eyes the history of the Hapsburgs, of Austria and of a part of Europe. Above each of the metal sarcophagi, which due to the ravages of time require constant restoration, hangs a name-plate. Here, in what for the most part are simple tombs set closely together, repose the remains of 144 Hapsburgs, today the symbols of a glorious past. To the right of the entrance, beginning from the Gründergruft (Crypt of the Founders), we immediately come upon the burial place of the Emperor Matthias and his wife Anna of Tyrol, then those of Ferdinand III, Leopold I and Joseph I. From this ancient crypt we go on to the room in which Maria Theresa and her husband Franz Stephan lie in a double Rococo tomb, the most beautiful in the Imperial crypt, by B. F. Moll. The last four rooms are the final resting places of Emperors Leopold II, Franz II, Ferdinand I of Austria and Maximilian of Mexico.

In the last crypt, facing the chapel before the exit, are the tombs of Franz Joseph, sovereign of the Austro-Hungarian Empire for 68 years, and those of his consort Elizabeth («Sissy») and their son Rudolf, who both died in tragic circumstances.

Following our visit to the Kaisergruft, we proceed down the Donnergasse, cross the Kärtnerstrasse and continue on the Himmelpfortgasse, where at No. 8 stands the **Stadtpalais des Prinzen Eugen** (Winter Palace of Prince Eugene), a Baroque masterpiece raised at the turn of the 18th century. Built by Fischer von Erlach the Elder and J. Lukas von Hildebrandt, the palace is today the seat of the Ministry of Finance. Very close by, at No. 6, is the Café Frauenhuber, founded by Maria Theresa's personal chef and patronized by Mozart and Beethoven.

FRANZISKANERKIRCHE

The Franciscan Church was built between 1603 and 1611 on the site of an earlier Franciscan convent: originally in Renaissance style, it was altered in the 18th century. The **interior** has a single nave and contains works by famous Baroque artists: the dramatic, phantasmagorical *high altar* (1707) is by Andrea Pozzo, while the artistically-carved *organ* (1642), in the choir behind it, is by J. Wöckert. At the center of the church square stands the *Mosesbrunnen* (Moses Fountain), a work by Johann Martin Fischer dating to 1798.

From the Franziskanerplatz, we cross the Singerstrasse and proceed down the Grünangergasse to the Domgasse. The block marked out by these streets and by the Blutgasse offers us one of the most outstanding examples of slum clearance in Vienna.

The Figarohaus and the noteworthy stuccoed ceiling of Mozart's studio. Below: the Basiliskenhaus in Schönlaterngasse.

Where until only a few years ago were reeking alleys and old houses there now rises a modern building complex with gardens, art galleries, shops and Kaffeehäusern (multi-storied coffee shops where one may stop for a while, read the newspapers and receive guests). At No. 5 of the Domgasse is the so-called **Figarohaus** (House of Figaro), where Mozart lived from 1784 through 1787 during his most creative period. It was here, as we are reminded by the plaque on the Schulerstrasse side, that he composed «The Marriage of Figaro» as well as other masterpieces. Today the apartment has been transformed into a small museum which preserves many objects that remind us of the great musician.

Only a few steps away is the Wollzeile, a long business street with many bookshops. At No. 5, in a passage leading through closed-in courtyards to Saint Stephan's Square, is the «Figlmüller», one of the most characteristic eating-places in Vienna.

At the level of No. 35 Wollzeile we turn into the Postgasse, where we find the Baroque **Dominikanerkirche** (Dominican Church), built in the 17th century by J. Spatz, C. Biasino and A. Canevale on the site of an older church. The Schönlaterngasse begins alongside the church.

Schönlaterngasse - Along this beautiful winding street we find many hospitable cafés and beer-houses and some true jewels of the art of ancient Vienna. No. 7 is the famous **Basiliskenhaus**, one of the oldest middle-class houses in the city; while dating to 1212, the building was much remodelled in the 16th and 17th centuries. Its name derives from a legend according to which a basilisk

was found in a well by the house; it would seem that a baker had the brilliant idea of killing it with a mirror - and in fact, upon seeing its ugliness, the monster exploded. The figure of the basilisk decorates the facade of the house. At No. 6 we note the **Schöne Laterne** (Pretty Lantern), forged in 1680, from which the street takes its name.

HEILIGENKREUZERHOF

The entrance to this immense courtyard, surrounded by beautiful 17th and 18th-century buildings, is at No. 5 of the Schönlaterngasse. For over 700 years it has been property of the monks of the Heiligenkreuz (Monastery of the Holy Cross, near Mayerling in Wienerwald).
Originally a city holding of the monastery, it was later transformed into a residential complex. The medieval look of the building has been all but obliterated, above all by the 17th- and 18th-century alterations which are responsible for its present-day look. Each of the buildings facing onto the large courtyard contributes in its own manner to creating the relaxing atmosphere that invites us to stop for a while. Of particular note is the Baroque **Bernhardskapelle**, (Chapel of Saint Bernard), the current aspect of which dates to about 1730. The altarpiece of the high altar is by M. Altomonte, the sculptures by Giovanni Giuliani, and the architectural frescoes by A. Tassi.

The Bernhardskapelle (Chapel of Saint Bernard).

Not far from the Heiligenkreuzerhof, closed in by three buildings of considerable historical and artistic interest, we find the beautiful **Dr. Ignaz-Seipel-Platz**, one of the focal points of the 1848 Revolution, which today bears the name of a Chancellor of the First Republic.
The **Jesuitenkirche** (Jesuit Church), with its facade delimited by two bell-towers, dominates the square. Built during the Counter-Reformation, it owes its richly decorated interior to Andrea Pozzo (early

A view of the Heiligenkreuzerhof.

Jesuitenkirche (Jesuit Church): the façade; the trompe l'oeil ceiling frescoes simulating the effect of a cupola; a view of the interior of the church.

18th century). The *High Altar* and the *ceiling frescoes* that create the trompe l'oeil effect of a cupola («Scheinarchitektur») are well worth seeing.

To the right of the church stands the **Akademie der Wissenschaften** (Academy of Sciences), a Rococo building by N. Jadot raised by order of Maria Theresa in the years 1753-1755. The facade, decorated with columns, statues and a large balcony, is also embellished by two exquisite fountains on the walls to the sides of the main entrance. In the interior, it is worthwhile visiting the beautiful *Aula Magna*, with frescoes by Gregorio Guglielmi; unfortunately, what we see are copies, since the originals were destroyed in the fire of 1961. The facing building is the **Alte Universität**, a 14th-century edifice restructured during the 17th century for the Jesuits who then directed the University.

From Dr. Ignaz-Seipel-Platz we turn into the **Bäckerstrasse**, with its many interesting buildings: at No. 7, a 16th-century Renaissance home with a lovely porticoed courtyard; at No. 8 and No. 16, two Baroque homes dating to the first half of the 18th century which display incontrovertible signs of the influence of the great architects of the age such as J. Lukas von Hildebrandt.

After having crossed a small square called **Lugeck**, at the center of which rises the monument to Gutenberg, we cross Rotenturmstrasse to the Hoher Markt.

HOHER MARKT

We may choose to visit the Roman ruins under the Hoher Markt, where we find the remains of homes of Roman officials dating to 100-300 AC along the main road that ran from east to west through the legionary castrum. Not far away, to the north, is the praetorium, headquarters of the Roman commander-in-chief. The Hoher Markt, devastated by bombing during World War II, has lost much of its fascination due to modern reconstruction. At its center is the Baroque **Vermählungsbrunnen** (Nuptial Fountain), built to a design by J. E. Fischer von Erlach in 1729-1732. The fountain is surmounted by

Hoher Markt: the Vermählungsbrunnen (Nuptial Fountain); below, the Ankeruhr (Anker Clock).

a bronze canopy supported by columns; on the base are the figures of the high priest celebrating the marriage of Mary and Joseph, and around them scenes from the life of Mary.

The right corner of the square hosts an interesting and singular work in Viennese Jugendstil style above an arch of the Rotgasse: the **Ankeruhr** (Anker Clock) created by F. Matsch in 1913. A figure from Austrian history glides across its face every hour; the spectacle at noon, when all 12 figures emerge, is enthralling.

ALTES RATHAUS

From the Hoher Markt, the Wipplingerstrasse takes us to this ancient building at No. 8, the seat of city government since 1316. It was transformed repeatedly in the centuries that followed until in 1885 the city functions were transferred to the Neues Rathaus on the Ring. The Baroque facade, added between 1699 and 1706, shows the influence of J. B. Fischer von Erlach. At the

center of the courtyard we see the beautiful **Andromeda-Brunnen** (Andromeda Fountain), the last work by G. R. Donner, dating to 1741: a small wrought-iron balcony juts over a high-relief, cast in lead, of Andromeda and Perseus killing the dragon. Across from the old Rathaus, at No. 7, is the **Böhmische Hofkanzlei** palace (Bohemian Court Chancery), a Baroque edifice built by J. B. Fischer von Erlach in 1714 and enlarged by M. Gerl in 1751. The portals with their caryatids and the beautiful statues on the facade, by Lorenzo Mattielli, merit attention. The rear of the palace looks out on the **Judenplatz**, at one time the center of the Jewish quarter.

The Andromeda-Brunnen (Andromeda Fountain). Above: the Altes Rathaus (on the left) and the Böhmische Hofkanzlei (Bohemian Court Chancery).

MARIA AM GESTADE

Proceeding along the Wipplingerstrasse and then turning to the right, we come shortly to the small church of Maria am Gestade (Saint Mary on the Bank). As its name suggests, the church was once on the bank of a secondary arm of the Danube. This church, our first, mention of which dates to 1158, was destroyed by the fire of 1262 and rebuilt. The Romanesque church owes its present-day look to plans by the

The Church of «Maria am Gestade»
(Saint Mary on the Bank).

Grand Ducal master-builder Michael Knab: the choir dates to
1330-1369, the nave and the upper portion of the tower to
1398-1414. This steeple, with its light filigreed stone cupola,
is the emblem of the church. In 1812, Emperor Franz I ordered restoration of the church after it had been used as stables and depot by Napoleon's troops.
Two splendidly painted panels of the original Gothic altar,
dating to about 1460 and among the most beautiful of their
time, hang at the two sides in front of the high altar, facing
the visitor. To the right is the *Coronation of the Virgin* (with
the *Crucifixion of Christ* on the back), to the left the *Annunciation* (with *Christ in the Olive Garden* on the back).
Other excellent examples of Gothic art include the figures on
the columns, sheltered by the elegant canopies; of special interest those of the Angel of the Annunciation and Maria, dating to about 1370. The panes of various of the church's windows, most of which date to the 14th century, have been re-
used in the choir and in the two windows of the south face of
the nave. The high altar, in Neo-Gothic style, was erected in
1845-1846.

A short walk along the Salvatorgasse (running the length of
the church and looking onto the rear of the old Rathaus) and
then down Marc Aurelstrasse brings us to the oldest part of
the city. Up a staircase and down the narrow Sterngasse, we

come to the **Fleischmarkt**, once Greek business district. Today it is studded with inns and beer halls. The famous «Griechenbeisl» , at No. 11, is situated in a medieval home that since the 15th century has been the preferred inn of many celebrated personalities.

RUPRECHTS-KIRCHE

From the Fleischmarkt, two short streets, the Rabengasse and the Seitenstettengasse (where the 18th-century Synagogue is located), lead to

«Maria am Gestade»: the panel-painting of the Annunciation *(ca. 1460) beside the high altar.*

an elegant, secluded terrace on which is found the Ruprechtskirche (Church of Saint Ruprecht), one of the oldest in Vienna.

Legend has it that the church was built by two disciples of Saint Ruprecht in the year 740. The nave and the lower portion of the bell-tower date to the 12th century. The Gothic presbytery was built following the fire of 1276 and the Gothic aisle was completed in 1436. Above the church, the simple exterior of which is ivy-clad, rises the Romanesque bell-tower with its windows with two lights. The two Gothic aisles of the **interior** house valuable works of art: the organ balustrade, dating to 1439 and, in the center window of the chancel, two

precious stained-glass panes from the late 13th century showing the *Crucifixion* and the *Virgin Enthroned*. The new stained glass work is by Lydia Roppolt.

The beautiful square surrounding the church looks out on the Franz-Josephs-Kai along the Donaukanal (Danube Canal); it can be reached by descending a staircase.

Ruprectskirche (Church of Saint Ruprecht).

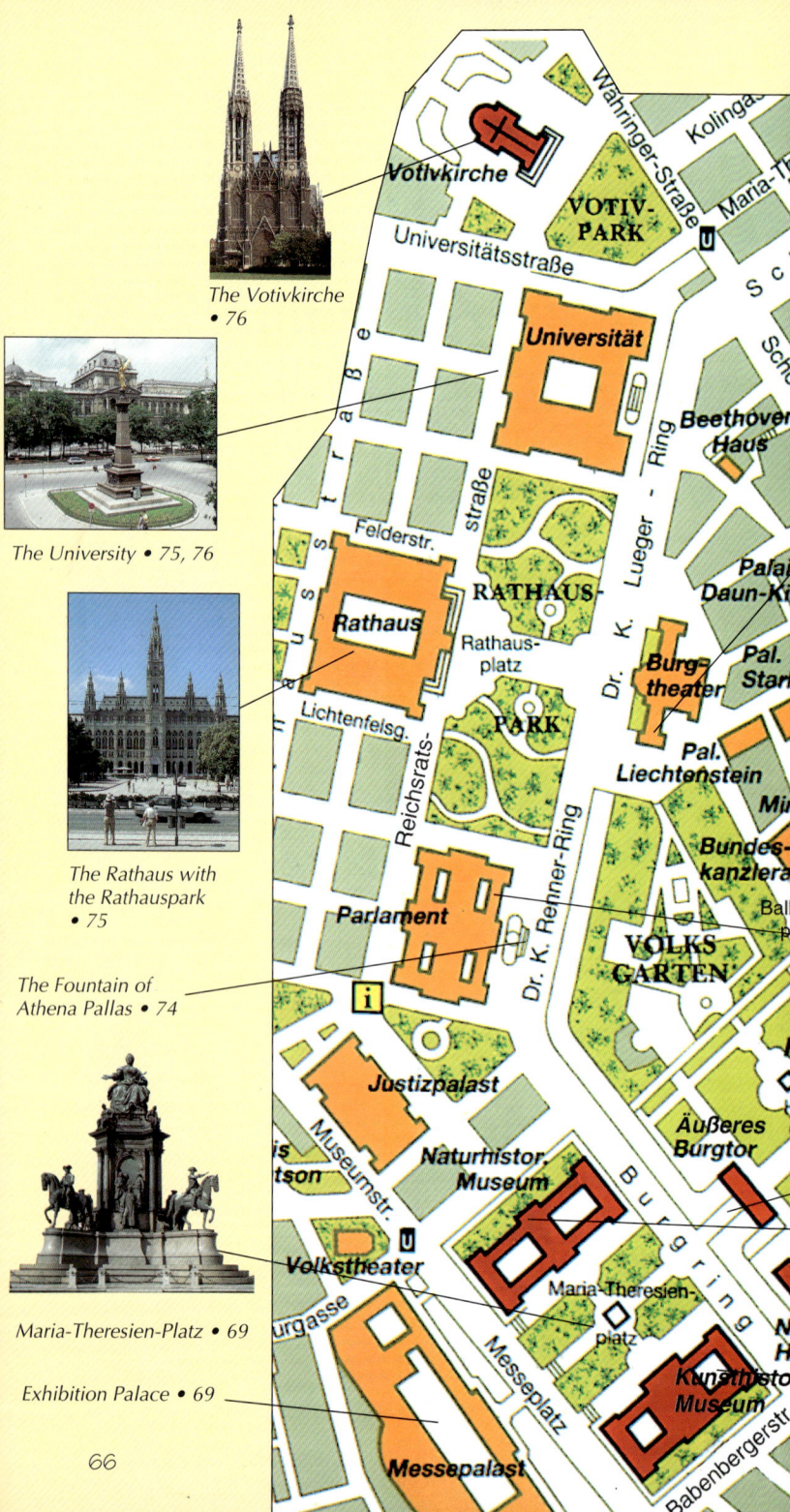

The Votivkirche • 76

The University • 75, 76

The Rathaus with the Rathauspark • 75

The Fountain of Athena Pallas • 74

Maria-Theresien-Platz • 69

Exhibition Palace • 69

Votivkirche

VOTIV-PARK

Universitätsstraße

Universität

Beethoven-Haus

Felderstr.

straße

RATHAUS-

Rathaus

Rathaus-platz

Palai Daun-Ki...

Burg-theater

Pal. Star...

Lichtenfelsg.

PARK

Pal. Liechtenstein

Parlament

Mir...

Bundes-kanzler...

Bal...

VOLKS-GARTEN

Justizpalast

Äußeres Burgtor

Naturhistor. Museum

Volkstheater

Maria-Theresien-platz

Messeplatz

Kunsthisto... Museum

Messepalast

Babenbergerstr.

Wahringer-Straße

Kolinga...

Maria-

Dr. K. Lueger - Ring

Dr. K. Renner-Ring

Reichsrats-

Museumstr.

urgasse

Burgring

66

The Burgtheater
• 74, 75

ITINERARY IV

Ringstrasse - Äusseres Burgtor - Maria-Theresien-Platz - Messepalast (Exhibition Palace) - **Kunsthistorisches Museum** (Museum of the History of Art) - Naturhistorisches Museum (Museum of Natural History) - Parliament - Pallas-Athene-Brunnen (Fountain of Athena Pallas) - **Burgtheater** - **Rathaus** (City Hall) - Rathauspark - Universität - Votivkirche - Minoritenplatz - Minoritenkirche (Church of the Friars Minor).

The Minoritenkirche,
Minoritenplatz
• 76, 77

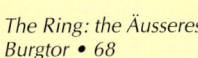

Parliament • 74

The Ring: the Äusseres
Burgtor • 68

Museum of Natural History
• 72, 73

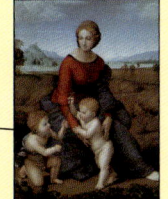

Museum of the
History of Art • 70/ 72

RINGSTRASSE

About 5 kilometers long and ca. 60 meters wide, this sumptuous boulevard (*Ring*), together with the Donaukanal, encloses the historical center of Vienna; it is divided into various sections, each with a different name: Stubenring, Parkring, Schubertring, Kärtnerring, Opernring, Burgring, Dr. Karl-Renner-Ring, Dr. Karl-Lueger-Ring and Schottenring.

In 1857, Emperor Franz Joseph ordered the demolition of the medieval walls that at the time still encircled the center of the city, and the ring road was built in place of the earlier bastions to serve that which was intended to become a capital city worthy of a great empire.

The Ringstrasse, commonly called simply "the Ring» , became the most important street in the city as soon as it was built. Along the grand artery were erected buildings for government and public administration, as well as noble residences and middle-class homes. A series of monumental works, squares, parks, monuments and gardens lend an extremely elegant cast to the whole. Despite the stylistic heterogeneity of its buildings, the Ring is lasting testimony to wealth and power. But it is an irony of fate that this grand boulevard, even while it was being built to symbolize the power and the grandeur of the Hapsburg Empire, was destined to witness its inevitable decline.

It is still today a special experience to travel the Ringstrasse on foot or in a Fiaker and to relive the pomp and the splendor of the past. The monumental character of the buildings imitates on a grand scale the examples of Classical antiquity, of the Renaissance, and of the Gothic style: the State Opera House, the Kunsthistorisches Museum and the Naturhistorisches Museum, the Burgtheater and the Burgtor, the Parliament, the Rathaus, the University, the Votivkirche and the Stock Exchange are the most important. And to these we must add the parks: the Stadtpark, the Burggarten, the Volksgarten, the Rathauspark and many others.

The most attractive part of the Ring begins at the Opera. From the Burgring, we may go through the **Äusseres Burgtor** (also Heldentor - Heroes' Gate) to reach the Heldenplatz and the Hofburg. The triumphal portal was built in 1824 in place of the ancient fortifications which were destroyed during Napoleon's siege of 1809. In 1934, a monument to the fallen was erected here.

A typical Viennese Fiaker.

Monument to Empress Maria Theresa.

MARIA-THERESIEN-PLATZ

This is one of the most striking points of the Ring: across from the Äusseres Burgtor, there opens out on the left the great square dedicated to Maria Theresa. Here, among flower-beds, lawns and fountains, there rise one facing the other the two buildings of the Kunsthistorisches Museum and the Naturhistorisches Museum, with their high domes and beautiful Neo-Renaissance facades decorated with columns and statues. The two museums were built between 1872 and 1881 by Gottfried Semper and Karl Hasenauer with the aim of grouping together the Imperial collections. In the interiors are halls frescoed by the most important artists of the age, such as Klimt, Makart and Munkáczy.

The great **Maria-Theresia-Denkmal**, completed in 1887 after 13 years of work, rises at the center of the square. At the feet of the Empress, whose enthroned figure reigns on the soaring monument, are represented the most important personalities of the time: on horseback, her generals, and standing, Kaunitz, Liechtenstein, Gluck, Haydn, Mozart and others who contributed to the glory of her empire. To the west of the square is the **Messepalast** (Exhibition Palace), a work by the two Fischer von Erlachs, built as Imperial stables between 1723 and 1725. The building, with its about 320 meters of facade, is today the Viennese center for exhibitions, trade fairs and fashion shows, but is destined to become a museum in the future. Almost hidden in its interior is the «Glacisbeisl», one of the celebrated Viennese *Beisln* (taverns).

The façade of the Kunsthistorisches Museum.

KUNSTHISTORISCHES MUSEUM

No differently from many other reigning dynasties, the Hapsburgs collected works of art of all kinds. Over the centuries, thousands of paintings and other art objects were continually added to the collections, which today form the nucleus of the Museum of the History of Art, home to one of the largest historical art collections in the world.

The visitor interested in art history simply cannot miss the innumerable masterpieces contained in this museum. On three floors, its 91 rooms exhibit four great collections: Egyptian art and art of the Classical Age, sculpture and the applied arts, the picture gallery and the coin cabinet.

Mezzanine - Immediately to the right of the foyer are the **Ägyptische Sammlung** (Egyptian Collection) and the **Antikensammlung** (Classical Collection), consisting of over 4000 works of art. Only a part of the collections is on display. **Room I**: The cult of the dead. **Room II**: The Orient; Pre-dynastic Egypt. **Room III**: The animal cults. **Room IV**: Writing. **Room V**: Late Egyptian sculptures and reliefs. **Room VI**: Everyday objects: fabrics, jewelry, tools, etc. **Room VIa**: *Tomb chamber of Prince Ka-Ni-Nisut* from Giza (ca. 2400 BC). **Room VII**: Middle and New Kingdoms: sculptures and reliefs. **Room VIII**: Old Kingdom: sculptures. **Room IX**: Cypriot sculptures and terra-cotta works. **Rooms X-XI**: Greek and Roman bronze sculptures (*Amazon Sarcophagus* and the *Youth* from Magdalenesberg). **Room XII**: Greek bronzes. **Room XIII**: The Etruscan Room. **Room XIV**: Greek vases and terracotta works. **Room XV**: Roman art: series of cameos dating from the 1st-3rd centuries AC, among which the famous 1st-century *Gemma Augustea* representing the apotheosis of Emperor Augustus. **Rooms XVI-XVII**: Byzantine and late medieval finds and 5th-century Germanic objects in gold. **Room XVIII**: *Treasure of Nagyszentmiklós*, also known as Attila's Treasure, consisting of 23 gold pieces (9th-century pre-Bulgarian art) found in Hungary (today Romania).

In the left wing is the rich **Sammlung plasticher Kunst und des Kunsthandwerks** (Collection of Sculpture and the Applied Arts). The museum also owns a splendid collection of 800 French and Flemish tapestries (Gobelin) which for reasons of conservation cannot be exhibited. **Rooms XIX-XX**: Works of Austrian Baroque and Rococo art, furniture, objects and ivory equestrian statues of three Hapsburg Emperors created by B. Steinle from 1662 to 1664. **Room XXII**: Baroque objects from Germany, Holland and Italy. **Room XXIV-XXV**: Vases in stone and precious metals from the 16th and 17th centuries and examples of the German goldsmiths' art. **Room XXVI**: *Saint Michael's goblet* in gold

Jane Seymour Queen of England. *Portrait by Hans Holbein the Younger (1536).*

Summer *by Arcimboldo (1563).*

and precious stones, of French origin, dated 1530. **Room XXVII**: *Bronzes* by Giambologna and Benvenuto Cellini's gold *Salt-Cellar*, dated 1540. **Room XXVIII**: German bronzes and intaglio and gold work from the 15th and 16th centuries. **Rooms XXIX-XXX**: Italian Renaissance bronzes and sculptures. **Room XXXII**: 15th-century Florentine sculpture: works by Della Robbia, Desiderio da Settignano (*Laughing Boy*) and Francesco Laurana (*Bust of Isabella of Aragon*, late 15th century). **Rooms XXXIV and XXXVI**: Medieval art, including the *Falconer* by Anton Pilgram, the *Madonna of Krumau* and the *Allegory of the Transience of Earthly Things* (dated ca. 1500). **Rooms XXXV and XXXVII**: 16th-century clocks and automata.

On the grand staircase leading to the first floor is the sculpture of *Theseus and the Centaur* by Antonio Canova.

First Floor - This astonishing collection is made up of about 1600 paintings by German, Flemish, Dutch, Italian, Spanish and French artists. **Room I**: Titian. **Cabinet 1**: Mantegna (*Saint Sebastian*), Antonello, Vivarini. **Room II**: Veronese. **Cabinet 2**: Bellini, Giorgione. **Room III**: Tintoretto, Bassano. **Cabinet 3**: Correggio, Parmigianino, Raphael. **Room V**: Caravaggio (*Madonna of the Rosary, David with the Head of Goliath*). **Cabinet 10**: Velázquez (*Portrait of the Infanta Margherita Theresa, Portrait of Filippo Prospero*). **Cabinet 11**: Carracci, Poussin, Rosa, Cortona. **Room VI**: Italian Baroque paint-

Madonna del Prato *by Raphael (ca. 1505).*

Hunters in the Snow *by Pieter Breughel the Elder (1565).*

ing: Reni, Guercino, Fetti, Giordano. **Cabinet 12**: Fetti, Strozzi, Cavallino. **Room VII**: Bellotto, Solimena, Tiepolo (*Death of Brutus*), Duplessis. **Cabinet 13**: Guardi, Canaletto. **Cabinet 14**: Bosch (*Christ Carrying the Cross*). **Room IX**: 16th-century Dutch painters. **Cabinet 15**: 15th and 16th-century Old Dutch Masters. **Room X**: This is the most valuable room in the entire Museum of the History of Art, containing the world's largest collection of works by Pieter Brueghel the Elder, one of the most famous masters of Flemish art (*Wedding Feast, Tower of Babel, Battle between Carnival and Lent, Hunters in the Snow, Children's Games, Calvary*). **Room XI**: Jordaens, Snyders. **Cabinet 17**: Danube School, Dürer, Cranach the Elder, Cranach the Younger. **Cabinet 18**: Holbein (*portraits*), Clouet. **Cabinet 19**: Aachen, Spranger, Arcimboldo, Brueghel. **Room XII**: Van Dyck (*The Fish Market*). **Cabinet 20**: Rubens (*Helene Fourment*). **Rooms XIII/XIV**: Rubens (*Saint Ildefonso Altarpiece, Altarpieces of the Altar of the Jesuits*). **Cabinet 21**: Teniers the Younger. **Cabinet 22**: Hals (*portraits*). **Room XV**: Rembrandt, Ruisdael, Van Goyen. **Cabinet 24**: Vermeer (*The Artist's Studio*), Gainsborough.

Second Floor - The **Münzkabinett** (Coin Cabinet), a numismatic collection of great value containing examples from every historical era, of which only 2000 are displayed, occupies certain of the rooms on this floor.

NATURHISTORISCHES MUSEUM

It was Franz Stephan I, husband of the Empress Maria Theresa, lover of the natural sciences and passionate collector, who laid the first stone of the minerals collection and procured many pieces which yet today form the nucleus of the collections of the Museum of Natural History. In 1889, Emperor Franz Joseph presided over the official inauguration of the museum, which in the meantime had been added to through acquisitions of the most disparate origins. Today the museum, with its 37 exhibit rooms, is one of the largest and the most important of its kind. Its eight sectors (mineralogy/petrography, geology/paleontology, the prehistorical collections, anthropology, botany and three zoology sections: vertebrates, insects and invertebrates) range over two floors.

Fossil frog of the Miocene era.

Mezzanine - The collection, exhibited in 19th-century showcases in lavishly frescoed rooms, is a true source of wonder. Valuable minerals, stones of gigantic sizes,

Maria Theresa's bouquet of gemstones.

meteorites, fossils and human skulls from 35,000 years ago alternate with many other interesting finds.

Rooms 1-5: A systematically-organized collection of minerals from all parts of the world, meteorites and precious stones, among which a topaz weighing 117 kilograms, the largest *platinum nugget* ever found (over 5 kg), a *salt obelisk* weighing 1680 kg, fragments of alexandrite of changing colors, a specimen of the *lunar rock* brought to Earth in 1972 by the «Apollo 17» astronauts; as well as diamonds of all kinds, gold nuggets and crystals of Japanese stibnite. In Room 4, that of the precious stones, we can admire the *bouquet of gems* (2700 in all) given in 1760 by Maria Theresa to her husband Franz Stephan I, and several Colombian emeralds of absolute purity. Room 5 contains the meteorite collection.

In **Rooms 6-10**, prehistoric flora and fauna illustrate the development of life on our planet during the Paleozoic, Mesozoic and Tertiary Eras. On exhibit in Room 6 are the oldest of the fossil plants; in Room 10, the impressive life-size reproductions of the enormous dinosaurs of the Mesozoic era (from 250 to 65 million years ago).

The **galleries near the staircase** house a large exhibit of finds from the Pleistocene glacial era (from 1,800,000 to 12,000 years ago), complete with exhaustive explanations of the causes and the spread of glaciation. Also on display are examples of European and American fauna.

Rooms 11-15: collection of Stone Age finds, including the famous *Venus of Willendorf*, a small fertility figure in calcareous stone (20-30,000 years old); Room 14 hosts an exhibit on the Hallstatt civilization (800-400 BC) which includes among other things a very beautiful and richly decorated hearse.

Rooms 16-17: Anthropology section. The many exhibits chart the evolution of man over the last 35,000 years.

Room 18 is dedicated to children and was designed to provide young visitors with an initiation to the natural sciences: many of the objects, instead of being protected by glass, are exhibited in hands-on displays that invite small visitors to touch in order to learn.

First Floor - In the botanical and zoological sections are exhibited a great number of finds as well as anatomical specimens of animals of both existing and extinct species.

Room 21: Ecology, an exhibit centering on the fundamental Laws of life on Earth.

Rooms 22-24 are dedicated to the invertebrates: there are thousands of mollusks, spiders, crustaceans and insects.

Rooms 25-39 are instead those of the vertebrates: fish, birds, amphibians, reptiles and mammals make up an immense, fantastic «inanimate» zoo. Among these, several species that are today threatened with extinction, including the Tasmanian wolf, the blue sheep and the Carolina parakeet.

The Venus of Willendorf.

PARLIAMENT

We need not be expert connoisseurs of art to recognize the artistic and cultural influences that inspired the architect Theophil Hansen in the design of this work: they are very evidently those of ancient Greece. The imposing entrance and the tall columns that support the tympanum

The Neo-classical façade of the Parliament building and the Pallas-Athene-Brunnen (Fountain of Athena Pallas).

are striking in their sheer grandiosity. The building was completed in 1883 and until 1918 was the seat of the Council of State. Since the proclamation of the Republic it has been the seat of both branches of the legislature: the Nationalrat (National Council) and the Bundesrat (Federal Council). A double ramp, embellished with statues of Greek and Roman historians, among whom Thucydides, Herodotus, Tacitus and Sallust, and by bronze sculptures of the Horse Tamers, leads to the entrance. In the square at the foot of the ramp stands the monumental **Pallas-Athene-Brunnen** (Fountain of Athena Pallas): the goddess of Wisdom, more than four meters tall, stands in a circle of allegorical figures; in her right hand is Nike, the goddess of Victory.

BURGTHEATER

Emperor Joseph II founded the Burgtheater in 1776 as the German National Theater. It was located in the Michaelerplatz until 1888, year in which its home became the new building on the Ring constructed after a plan by Gottfried Semper. The Burgtheater has always been one of the most important German-language prose stages. As is the case with many other important buildings in Vienna, the theater suffered heavy damage during the last war, but painstaking restoration and enlargement work has restored it at least in part to its ancient splendor. On the side staircases, spared by the bombs, are some notable *paintings* by G. Klimt and F. Matsch. Of the many Viennese prose theaters, this is the most famous. During the season, which runs from September to June, at least 15 theaters are active in Vienna, offering a wide range of productions of both classical and modern works.

The Burgtheater, one of the most prestigious theaters worldwide.

To name just a few of the most well-known: the Akademietheater, the Theater in der Josefstadt and the Volkstheater.

RATHAUS

On the tower of the Neues Rathaus (City Hall), at 103 meters height, an iron horseman («eiserner Rathausmann») armed with sword and banner stands guard over the fate of the city.

The Neo-Gothic Neues Rathaus (City Hall) with the Rathauspark.

Seat of the Mayor's offices and of the City Council, it is one of the most important Neo-Gothic buildings in Vienna. It was built between 1972 and 1883 by Friedrich von Schmidt. The facade of the building is distinguished by four side towers and the high center tower on which the *Rathausmann* stands: the statue, 3.4 meters tall and weighing almost 4 tons, is a work by the master ironsmith Alexander Nehr; not only is it the emblem of Vienna, but it also acts as a lightning rod! Many rooms in the interior are open to the public; for example, the Schmidt room, the City Council meeting room, which boasts a great bronze chandelier 10 meters in height and 254 lamps, and the great entertainment hall (Festsaal).One of the interior courtyards, the **Arkadenhof**, hosts the open-air concerts of the summer music festival.

In front of the building, the shady, well-kept **Rathauspark** looks out on the Ring. Under exotic trees, each supplied with a plaque with its name, among fountains and groups of benches, are many statues and monuments; one of these is dedicated to the kings of the waltz, Johann Strauss the Elder and Josef Lanner. Along the boulevard that leads from the Rathaus to the Burgtheater are eight more statues of important figures in Austrian history.

UNIVERSITÄT

A short distance from the Rathauspark, on Dr. Karl-Lueger-Ring, there arises the massive University building in Neo-Renaissance style built by Heinrich von Ferstel in the years 1873-1883.

The Neo-Renaissance University building.

The University of Vienna, founded in 1365 by Archduke Rudolf IV, is one of the oldest in central Europe. It was reorganized and enlarged during the illuminat-

The Votivkirche.

ed dominion of Maria Theresa, and since 1848, following the reform implemented by the then Minister of Education Count Thun, has become a university with thousands of students who dedicate their time to their studies in monumental halls.

Of particular note are the great Aula Magna and the beautiful arcaded courtyard, a true visual delight: a wide colonnade, decorated with the busts of illustrious professors who in the past taught in Vienna, surrounds 3000 square meters of lawns studded with trees; at the center is the **Kastaliabrunnen** (Kastalia Fountain) created in 1910 by E. Hellmer.

VOTIVKIRCHE

Like any reigning family, the Hapsburgs were the target of frequent assassination attempts. On this site, in 1853, the young Emperor Franz Joseph escaped death in an attempt on his life; his brother Maximilian, future Emperor of Mexico, ordered a church erected as a sign of thanks. Designed by Heinrich von Ferstel, who took his inspiration from the great French Gothic cathedrals of the 13th century, the Votivkirche was the first post-Baroque church in Vienna. Two bell-towers, each 99 meters in height, rise at the sides of the facade, which is embellished by a sumptuous portal.

The idea was that of building a temple celebrating illustrious Austrians, similar to London's Westminster Abbey, but the program was brought to fruit only in part: since 1945, the stained-glass windows of the left aisle have portrayed socially-committed personalities and in the chapel of the baptismal font only one of the planned funerary monuments, that of Niklas Salm, defender of Vienna during the first Turkish siege of 1529, has been erected.

MINORITENPLATZ

If we go around the back of the Burgtheater in the direction of the Hofburg, we will come to the Minoritenplatz (Minorite Square), a noble square in which an important part of city political life unwinds. At No. 3 we see the 17th-century

Palais Dietrichstein, transformed in 1755 by L. F. Hillebrand, today seat of the Foreign Ministry. At No. 4 stands **Palais Liechtenstein** (the winter residence of the noble family), with a beautiful side door by an unknown artist. Built to plans by Enrico Zuccalli and Domenico Martinelli in the years 1694-1706, the palace still belongs to the family. At No. 5, the **Palais Starhemberg**, today seat of the Ministry of Education and Sciences. Count Starhemberg, defender of Vienna during the Turkish siege of 1683, died here in 1701.

MINORITENKIRCHE

Begun in 1339, the Church of the Friars Minor was completed only at the end of the century. Badly damaged during the two Turkish sieges, the church was restored and transformed in Baroque style, but work in 1784-1789 by Ferdinand von Hohenberg restored all of its interior to the original Gothic style.

The church is set at the center of the square and has a high, sloping roof; on the facade is the important **Hauptportal** (Main Portal), work of the Parisian monk Jacob. The interior is divided by 8 columns into a nave and two aisles; in the left aisle is an exceptional mosaic, weighing 20 tons: a full-size reproduction of the *Last Supper* by Leonardo da Vinci, executed by Giacomo Raffaelli in the years 1806-1814.

Above: an Atlas at the side entrance to Palais Liechtenstein.
The Minoritenkirche and its interior.

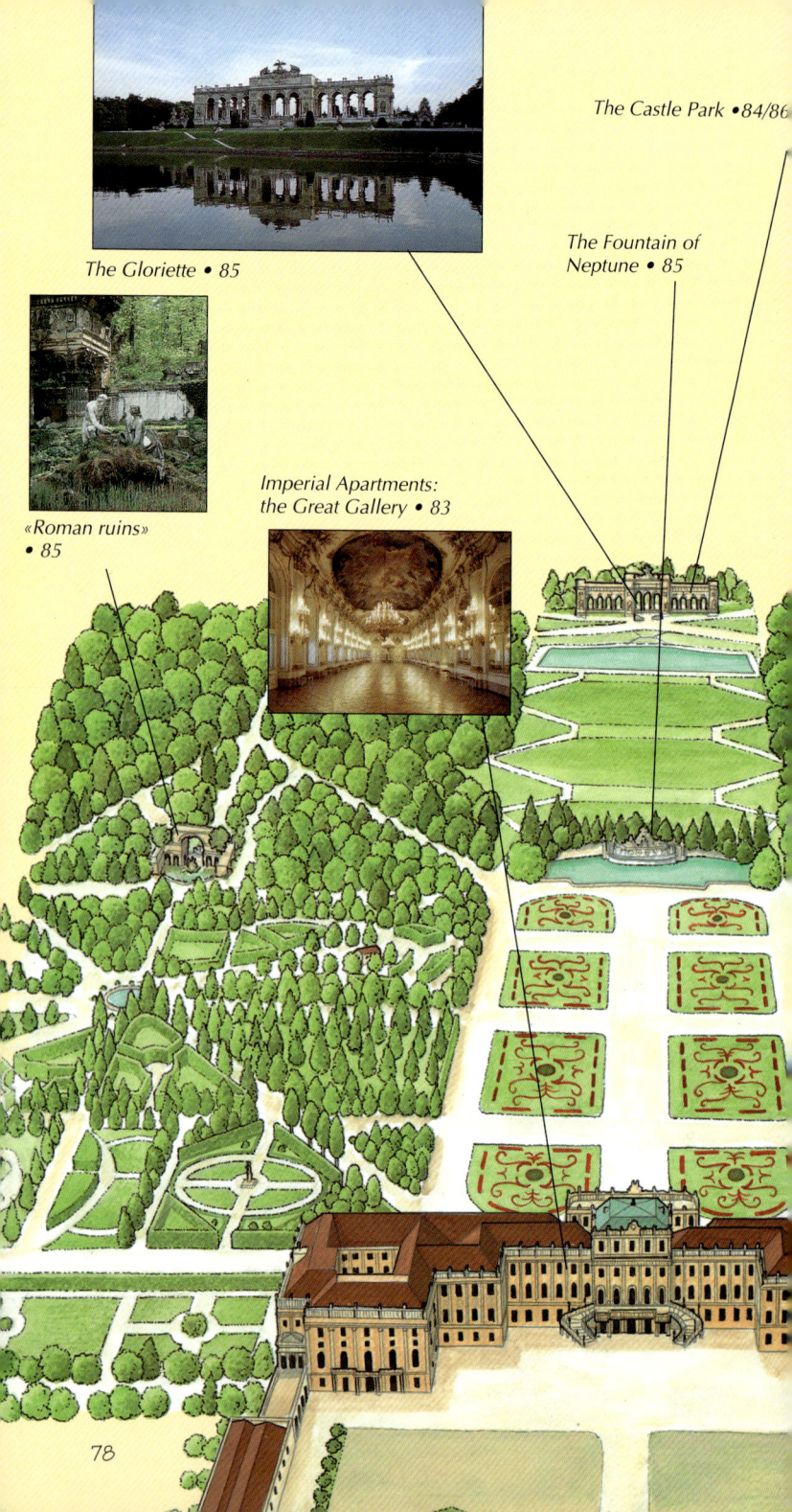

The Gloriette • 85

«Roman ruins» • 85

Imperial Apartments: the Great Gallery • 83

The Castle Park • 84/86

The Fountain of Neptune • 85

The Palm House • 86

he Main Pavilion
86

ITINERARY V

Schloss Schönbrunn (Schönbrunn Castle) - **Kaiserliche Appartements** (Imperial Apartments) - **Park** - Botanischer Garten (Botanical Garden) - Palmenhaus (Palm House) - **Wagenburg** (Imperial Coach Museum) - Technisches Museum (Technical Museum).

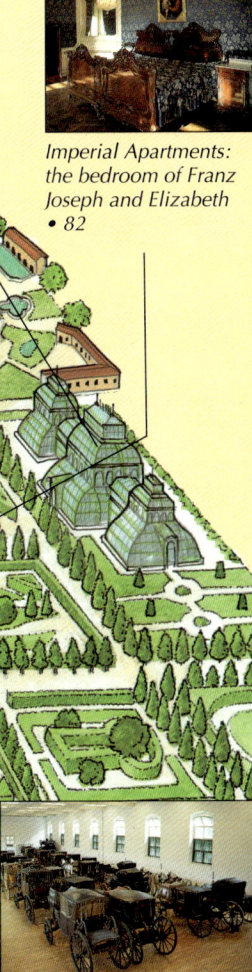

Imperial Apartments: the bedroom of Franz Joseph and Elizabeth • 82

Imperial Coach Museum • 86, 87

Schönbrunn Castle in a painting by Bernardo Bellotto (1759/60).

SCHLOSS SCHÖNBRUNN

Try to imagine a long line of splendid carriages conveying the members of the Imperial family from the Hofburg to their summer residence, the lively activity of maids and servants upon their arrival, and perhaps even the Empress' stroll, with her ladies-in-waiting, through the park of the Schönbrunn Castle. But if your imagination falls short, paintings by Canaletto (B. Bellotto) from the mid-18th century can help suggest the atmosphere of that which was once the Versailles of Austria. Even if it is perhaps not the most beautiful of the Austrian castles, Schönbrunn is undoubtedly the most famous.

Today, Schönbrunn can be reached from the center of Vienna, via underground, in just a few minutes. The station, a Jugendstil work by Otto Wagner, is right at the entrance to the castle, which is distinguished by two obelisks topped by the Imperial eagle.

A SHORT HISTORY OF THE CASTLE

Towards the middle of the 16th century, Emperor Maximilian II acquired a small hunting castle, the Katterburg, surrounded by extensive woodlands and fields; it was transformed by Maximilian himself and later by his successors. Unfortunately, the course of history was not clement to certain types of development: both the castle and the park were totally destroyed in 1683 by the Turks during the second siege of Vienna. Following the rout of the invaders, Emperor Leopold I charged the architect J. B. Fischer von Erlach with designing a grand castle just outside the city. The draft plan (1692/1693) surpassed all expectations: on the hill where today we see the Gloriette there was to have arisen a castle even larger

Schönbrunn Castle: the façade overlooking the garden.

than Versailles, the symbol of the powerful French monarchy and often object of envy by the Hapsburgs. But the wars had dried up the state treasuries, and Fischer von Erlach was forced to scale down his plans. In 1695 construction of the castle we see today was begun.

Work dragged on for decades, until in 1743 Empress Maria Theresa employed Nikolaus Pacassi to complete the castle, adapting the original plans to the taste of the times.

The Empress and her 16 children used Schönbrunn as their permanent residence and lent to the park and the castle itself their own personal touch. Joseph II, son of Maria Theresa, held little store by the pomp that had so attracted his mother and concentrated his interest mainly on the park. It was during his reign that the botanical garden and the zoological garden were inaugurated. During the centuries that followed, the Schönbrunn bore witness to dramatic events: in the years 1805 and 1809 it was used as headquarters by Napoleon; and it was here that the capitulation of Austria was signed. After Napoleon's fall, his son, the «King of Rome», born of Napoleon's marriage to Maria Luisa, lived here as though in exile until he died of tuberculosis in 1832. From 1848 until the end of the long reign of Franz Joseph, the castle was used as the Imperial summer residence. On 11 November 1918, Karl I of Hapsburg signed his abdication here, so ending the centuries-long dominion of the Hapsburgs and paving the way to the Republic. And Schönbrunn has been witness to great international events even in more recent times: the historic East-West summit meeting between John F. Kennedy and Nikita Khrushchev, on 3 June 1961, is an example.

THE CASTLE

*As we near Schönbrunn, the castle appears as a wide, long and not very high construction of a color known as Schönbrunn yellow or Imperial yellow. A beautiful wrought-iron Rococo gate, with an obelisk at either side, opens into the grandiose **Ehrenhof** (Court of Honor), a large open area sur-*

The Imperial Apartments of
Schönbrunn:

The bedroom of Franz Joseph
and Elizabeth.
Below: the Rösselzimmer, or
«Hall of the Horses».
The bedroom of Emperor
Franz Joseph.

rounded on three sides by buildings, where military reviews
and open-air entertainments were held in the 18th century.
On the right is the small but quite magnificent **Schlosstheater**,
inaugurated in 1747 and modified in 1766-1767 by Ferdinand von Hohenberg, where summer performances are still
held. Haydn directed here in 1777, Mozart in 1786.
At the center of the rather linear facade, flanked by columns,
is the entrance to the Imperial apartments and to the park.

Kaiserliche Appartements - Of the 1400 rooms in the castle,
only 45 are accessible to the public (guided tours in various
languages are available). These rooms give us an idea of the
style of life of the Hapsburgs and of the taste of the times:

Maria Theresa's love for the
exotic, Franz Joseph's sobri-
ety, and the luxury of the
public reception halls. The
Rococo decorations characteristic of these interiors are
by Nikolaus Pacassi. The
two very beautiful majolica
heating stoves were fired by
the servants from the en-
trance so as not to disturb
Their Highnesses.
Our visit to the apartments
begins with the 10 rooms of
the **apartment of Franz
Joseph**: the Emperor was famous for his Spartan lifestyle
and his refusal to accept in-
novation. It is even said that
he protested the installation
of electric power in the castle. His extremely sober per-
sonality is also mirrored in
the furnishings: the camp-bed
we see here is that in which
he died on 21 November

The Great Gallery in Schönbrunn Castle.

1916. In striking contrast, the public reception halls and the **apartment of Maria Theresa**, where luxury and pomp unite to create an unequalled richness, are the overt expression of a great woman and a powerful empire.

Tapestries, porcelains, chandeliers, rare pieces of Chinese and Japanese art and furnishings in valuable woods fill these rooms. Worth special attention are the **Hall of Mirrors**, where Mozart, still a child, gave a concert for Maria Theresa; the **Vieux-Laque-Zimmer**, the walls of which are decorated with exquisite oriental lacquered panels that were painted on the high sea to avoid dust marring the surfaces; the **Chinese Rooms**, often used for secret political meetings and private discussions, with precious *Ming porcelains*; the **Porcelain Room**, the wooden panelling of which creates the effect of porcelain; the **Milionen-Zimmer**, called thus due to the high cost of its decoration in precious wood (ficatin) brought from Guiana and the Antilles, and to the precious 16th-century *Indian and Persian miniatures* it houses; the **Great Gallery**, 43 meters in length, which was used for banquets, court entertainments and important meetings.

To the left of the entrance are the **Bergl-Zimmer**, frescoed with floral motifs, figures of animals and tropical plants by Johann Bergl in 1769-1777. The rooms, open from May through September, were the favorite retreat of Maria Theresa during the heat of summer; the Crown Prince Rudolf later lived here.

![The Gloriette]

The Gloriette.

Fountains in the castle park.

Park - The **Schlosspark** has an even more grandiose aspect than the castle: with its oft-times restructured 1.6 square kilometers, covering almost the same area as Vienna's first Bezirk (*Innere Stadt*), it loses nothing by comparison with French models. It is the ideal setting for a relaxing stroll after our visit to the Castle rooms. As we walk slowly down the shady lanes, among high espalier hedges that conceal fountains and Roman ruins, it is easy to become enchanted with the romantic at-

mosphere; Baroque pavilions and statues follow one another over the lawns and under the trees, from which playful squirrels look out in the hope of scrounging nuts from visitors.

Upon entering the park, our attention is drawn by the **Gloriette**, the elegant Neo-Classical arcade that dominates the low hill south of the castle. It was built, together with many other parts of the park, by Ferdinand von Hohenberg in 1775 in remembrance of the Austrian victory over the Prussians in 1757 at Kolin. The Gloriette, 19 meters in height and 95 meters wide, decorated with trophies, animal skulls and armor, is the best vantage point for enjoying the panorama of the castle and the park, as it offers a view that sweeps over the entire city. And so it is imperative to climb the gently-sloping hill and to linger near the elegant flower-beds that are re-planted three times a year (in spring, they all boast Dutch tulips). Below the great flower-beds, at the foot of the hill, is the monumental **Neptun-brunnen** (Fountain of Neptune), dating to 1780, a worthy conclusion to the lower part of the park.

From the Gloriette, to the right facing the castle, a path through a wooded area leads us to imitation Roman ruins and to the **Schöner Brunnen**, the «beautiful fountain» from which both the castle and the park took their names. Returning to the avenue along the flower-beds, we reach the entrance to the **Schönbrunn Zoological Gardens**, built in 1752 by Franz Stephan of Lorraine, consort of Maria Theresa, and later expanded by their son Joseph II: this is the world's only example of a Baroque zoo. The original structure had become the object of continual repairs; over the last few years a goodly portion of the zoo has been renovated according to contemporary criteria in order to provide better living conditions for its thousands of animal guests. Not far away is another jewel of the Schönbrunn park: the **Botanischer Garten** (Botanical Garden) with its **Palmenhaus** (palm greenhouse), the largest of its kind in Europe, built of wood and metal by the architect F. von Segenschmid in 1880. In the midst of flower-beds, the stat-

ues of Franz I and Joseph II as well as a sundial adorn a delightful corner of the garden which is generally the milieu of children but also of elderly ladies in search of sun and repose.

Wagenburg - In the right wing of the Schönbrunn castle, with its entrance on the Ehrenhof, is the museum exhibiting Imperial coaches and carriages in what was once the castle coach-house. This is the largest collection of vehicles used on State occasions and for pleasure by the Viennese Court between 1690 and 1918. There are coronation coaches, hearses, hunting and travelling carriages as well as precious

The Palmenhaus (Palm House).

trappings and harnesses. Of special note: the 18th-century **Imperial coronation coach**, **Empress Elizabeth's funeral coach** and the gig built to order for Napoleon's son.

The Main Pavilion of the castle park.

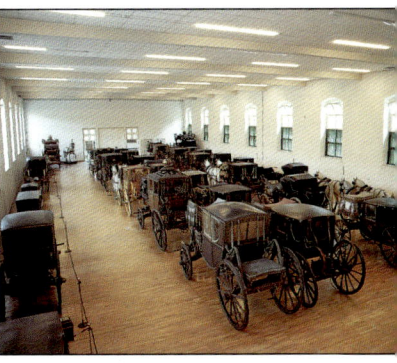

The departure of the royal couple, Franz Joseph and Elizabeth, in a painting in the Wagenburg (ca. 1855).

Coaches and drays in the Imperial Coach Museum.

A few hundred meters from the Schönbrunn castle, at No. 212 at the top of Mariahilfer-Strasse, stands the **Technisches Museum** (Technical Museum): in a three-story building, this museum offers a panorama on the world of technology and industry and on the contribution by Austrian scientists to their development. Among many other exhibits, here is found the first sewing machine (Madersperger, 1830), the oldest typewriter (Mitterhofer, 1860), Cugnot's steam-driven vehicle (1770) and one of the Wright brothers' first airplanes (1903).

The Museum is currently closed for restauration.

The Imperial coronation coach.

The Postparkasse building
• 99, 100

Museum of Applied Arts (MAK) • 99,100

The Great Marble Hall
• 93, 96

Stadtpark: the Johann Strauss monument
• 98, 99

Prater • 100, 101

The Wienflussportal pavilion • 98, 99

The main staircase • 96

Museum of 19th- and 20th-Century Art • 96, 97

Unteres Belvedere (Lower Belvedere) - Österreichisches Barockmuseum (Museum of Austrian Baroque Art) - **Belvedere Park** - **Oberes Belvedere** (Upper Belvedere) - Österreichische Galerie des 19. und 20. Jahrhunderts (Museum of 19th- and 20th-Century Art) - Stadtpark - Kursalon - Wienflussportal (Portal of the River Wien) - **Museum für Angewandte Kunst** (Austrian Museum of Applied Arts) - Postsparkasse (Austrian Post Office Savings Bank) - Urania - **Prater**.

One of the sphinxes in the Belvedere Park • 92, 93

Museum of Austrian Baroque Art • 91, 92

The statue of Prince Eugene • 92

BELVEDERE CASTLE

HISTORICAL OVERVIEW

In 1683, the Turks laid siege to Vienna for the second time and, as in 1529, the defence of the city became the symbol of Christian resistance against Ottoman expansionism. Even Prince Eugene of Savoia rushed to the aid of the besieged city, offering his services to Emperor Leopold. There thus began a long and glorious series of battles and victories that made the Prince a well-loved figure throughout the Empire - and one feared by the enemy. He was even supported by the Viennese population when the Emperor attempted to remove him from his position as commander-in-chief of the Imperial armed forces. In that era of glorious wars, Baroque art reached its climax. Its representative powers made it an ideal medium for personifying power, pomp and splendor and the dominion of absolutism. Even Prince Eugene decided to build a residence for himself near Vienna, of a splendor by no means inferior to that of the Hapsburg royal palace, as a means of confirming his political position. At the same time, every important Baroque building erected meant an alteration to the medieval image of the city; over the decades, this took place to an ever greater degree, until Vienna, from that sort of medieval fortress it had been, became a great Imperial Residence.

And thus, in 1714-1716, there was erected the Lower Belvedere, the castle/residence of Prince Eugene. J. Lukas von Hildebrandt, one of the most important architects of the time and the designer of many of the Baroque buildings in Vienna, made of the Belvedere a true masterpiece.

At the turn of the 18th century the layout of the Baroque garden was begun; and at the highest point in this panorama of pools and planted beds, Hildebrandt erected the Upper Belvedere in two short years (1721-1722). Following the death of Prince Eugene, the castle passed to the Hapsburgs and in the early years of the 20th century was the residence of the heir to the throne, Archduke Franz Ferdinand, whose assassination in Sarajevo sparked World War I.

Facing page: the Lower Belvedere (Unteres Belvedere).
The main façade (above) and that overlooking the garden.

Panorama of Vienna from the Upper Belvedere (Oberes Belvedere).

Unteres Belvedere - The Belvedere Complex is made up of two buildings separated by the grandiose, gently-sloping and elegantly designed park. The Lower Belvedere, at the base of the rise, was terminated in 1716 as the residence of Prince Eugene: two simple, low facades conceal a luxurious interior with a series of halls decorated in accordance with the Baroque taste of the era. The **Marble Hall**, frescoed by Martino Altomonte and Gaetano Fanti with scenes celebrating the moments of glory in the life of the Prince, merits special attention. To the right of the entrance to the Lower Belvedere is the museum.

Österreichisches Barockmuseum - The Museum of Austrian Baroque Art has found its ideal setting in these 9 rooms, and it contains a complete collection of the most important artists and currents in art in the Austria of the 17th and 18th centuries: among the most renowned are J. M. Rottmayr, M. Altomonte, P. Troger, D. Gran, M. J. Schmidt, G. R. Donner, A. Maulpertsch and F. X. Messerschmidt. Donner was the author of the sculptures adorning the Marble Hall and the

Lower Belvedere: the Goldkabinett (or «Hall of Mirrors») with the statue of Prince Eugene by Balthazar Permoser (1721).
Below: one of the sphinxes in the garden.

Yellow Hall, while those with comic faces, like the «Coward», the «Jester» and the «Fool», in the Marble Gallery, are the work of Messerschmidt. The museum also houses the lead originals of the statues decorating the Donnerbrunnen (Providentia Fountain) in the Neuer Markt, which represent *Providence* and the four rivers *Enns, March, Traun* and *Ybbs.*

Around to the right of the Lower Belvedere we find the Orangery, where sculptures and panels by Roland Frueauf the Elder (15th century) and works by other artists are on exhibit in the Gothic section of the Museum Mittelalterlicher Österreichischer Kunst (Museum of Austrian Medieval Art).

Garden - No great Baroque castle could be considered complete without its park, with a great number of pools, statues, hedges and avenues and paths, in line with the taste of the period. The architectural geometry of the gardens was subject to strict rules. The garden is the work of Dominique Girard (1717): it

Lower Belvedere: Character Heads *by Franz Xavier Messerschmidt.*

includes three broadly terraced lawns with fountains, cascades, flights of steps and statues of figures from Greek mythology that rise to the facade of the Upper Belvedere. A pleasant walk through this fascinating scenario takes us to the Upper Belvedere, which offers a splendid view of Vienna with the Lower Belvedere in the foreground.

Oberes Belvedere - Prince Eugene's summer residence could not have had a more resplendent setting, and here Hildebrandt's artistic expression of the Baroque reached its apex. A long building, with projections and recesses and three series of large windows, it is a convincing statement of harmony and elegance. The Upper Belvedere was not merely a palace for official use; it was also to host great celebrations and entertainments. The entrance hall is of imposing aspect, with its vaults supported by four figures of Atlas which give the impression of holding the weight of the entire building on their shoulders. Off the entrance there open a series of salons and the richly decorated staircase leading to the first floor. Here we find the **Chapel**, with frescoes by Carlo Carlone, and the **great Marble Hall**. It was in this hall that on 15 May 1955 the four occupying powers and Austria, which guaranteed its independence and neutrality, signed the Austrian State Treaty. In the hall is a painting immortalizing the historic event, which was a true miracle of

Lower Belvedere: the bedroom of Prince Eugene.

Upper Belvedere: the façade on the garden.
Preceding pages: Upper Belvedere. The main façade.

diplomacy of the Cold War: the protagonists of the international political scene of the time are easily recognizable.
On summer evenings, from May through September, classical «son et lumière» presentations are held, with music, lights and sound illustrating the fascinating history of the castle and the story of its Prince.

Österreichische Galerie des 19. und 20. Jahrhunderts - The Upper Belvedere today houses an important art gallery containing paintings and sculptures that give us a general idea of the development and flowering of art between the late 19th

Upper Belvedere: the Great Marble Hall.

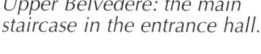

Upper Belvedere: the main staircase in the entrance hall.

and early 20th centuries. The artists of the Sezession and their art have here been given the prominence they deserve. The Sezession artistic movement had begun to develop in open contrast with the official currents in the art of the time. Romako, Makart and Schindler expressed official artistic leanings; Klimt, Schiele, Kokoschka, Moser, Gerstl and Hannak are instead only a few of the artists presented in this interesting gallery. On the first floor are exhibited portraits and landscapes by painters of the Biedermeier era (F. G. Waldmüller, F. v. Amerling, J. Alt, R. v. Alt, F. Gauermann and others) besides small paintings by Adalbert Stifter. On the second floor are Sezession paintings and sculptures through 1945 (Klimt, Schiele, Kokoschka, Boeckl). The works in the Schiele and Klimt collections are quite numerous.

Judith *by Gustav Klimt (1904).*

Portrait of Sonia Knips
by Gustav Klimt (1898).

Corpus Christi Morning
by F. G. Waldmüller (1857).

The Kursalon in the Stadtpark. Below: the monument to Johann Strauss and the Pavilion of the Wienflussportal (Wien River Gate).

STADTPARK

Opened to the public in 1862, this was the first of Vienna's city parks. On its lawns and along the bank of the river Wien are numerous monuments to famous musicians such as *Anton Bruckner* and *Franz Schubert*; the most imposing monument is that dedicated to the *king of waltzes, Johann Strauss*, a work by E. Hellmer. A charming little lake, inhabited by ducks and swans, adorns the center of the park. At the westernmost end of the Stadtpark, in the **Kursalon**, an orchestra plays

MAK - Austrian Museum of Applied Arts: Biedermier Imperial Hall, created by Jenny Holzer.

the famous Viennese waltzes every evening from March through October. Strolling along the riverbank, we come to the interesting **Wienflussportal** (Portal of the River Wien), a Jugendstil work by F. Ohmann from 1903-1906.

MUSEUM FÜR ANGEWANDTE KUNST

The Austrian Museum of Applied Arts, built in the years spanning 1868 and 1871, is the oldest of its kind on the European continent. The thousands of pieces of furniture, objects for everyday use, glass, ceramics, rugs and other items on exhibit in this building on the Stubenring bear mute witness to the high artistic value of handcrafts in different historical periods and in different parts of the globe. Renovation of the MAK exhibits was conducted in collaboration with artists of international fame, who laid out the traditional contents of the collection in a contemporary context.

The Postsparkasse building.

The exhibits are parcelled out among 10 rooms according to the styles of the different ages:
Romanesque,Gothic, Renaissance – Baroque, Rococo – Classicism – Empire, Biedermeier – Historicism, Jugendstil – Oriental Art – Wiener Werkstätte – Jugendstil, Art Déco – Contemporary Art – Eastern Asia.

All the sections feature study rooms, open to the public, that integrate the exhibit rooms.

The valuable MAK collection of glass and porcelain objects, fabrics, rugs, furniture and other objects from the Viennese crafts studios is exhibited in an attractive modern setting.

From the MAK, past the Stubenring and across to the other bank of the Danube; down Praterstrasse to the Prater. Along the way we find two important Jugendstil buildings. In Georg-Coch-Platz, to the left of the Ring, rises the tall and massive **Postsparkasse** building (Austrian Post Office Savings Bank), a work by the well-known architect Otto Wagner dating from 1904-1905; it was completely renovated in the 1970s and is a typical example of functional architecture: the banking hall is quite interesting. Not far from the Postsparkasse, on the bank of the Donaukanal where the Aspernbrücke unites the first Bezirk (Innere Stadt) with the second Bezirk (Leopoldstadt), is the **Urania** building, built in 1910 by Otto Wagner's protégé Max Fabiani: the Urania is an institute of the Popular University of Vienna with various halls for conferences and movie projection; the tower is home to an astronomical observatory.

PRATER

Not far from the center of the city is the Prater, which can be reached by public transport.

In 1560, Emperor Maximilian II transformed this broad stretch of land between the Danube and the Donaukanal into a hunting preserve for exclusive use by the Court and the aristocracy. Two centuries later, in 1766, the illuminated reformer Emperor Joseph II transformed it into an enormous park accessible to the entire population. In just a few years the Prater became the favorite recreation spot for the Viennese. Booths and attractions of all kinds sprang up in ever greater numbers, cafés were opened ... and the image of this great extension of woods and meadows was inevitably changed. In the 19th century and until the fall of the Monarchy, the Prater was patronized by Viennese of every social extraction. Following its decline during the crisis period spanning the two World Wars and culminating in the destruction wreaked in 1945, the Prater has today regained all its ancient charm. Sports facilities of all kinds and innumerable attractions stand out against a splendid natural setting.

From the **Praterstern**, the vast square at the entrance to the Prater at which the underground also stops, arises the main boulevard (**Hauptallee**) that divides the Prater in two parts for the five kilometers of its length; at the top of the avenue, on the left, is the **Wurstelprater** (amusement park) with its many cafés and restaurants: a true mecca of rides and booths selling toys and sweets. It is here that one of the symbols of Vienna, the **Riesenrad** (Ferris Wheel), rises to the spectacular height of 67 meters. The 15 cars move slowly, at a speed of 75 cm/second, to offer us the opportunity to savor an «aerial» view of the city. The wheel was built in 1897 by the Englishman W. Hitchins, who had previously designed similar wheels for Chicago, London, Blackpool and Paris (none of which is still standing). Close by the enormous wheel is the **Pratermuseum**, with its collection of items salvaged from the old amusement park, razed in 1945.

Not far from the museum are sports facilities of all kinds, among which the well-known Vienna Stadium (Ernst-Happel-Stadion).

On these pages: attractions in the amusement park on the Wurstelprater, with the famous Riesenrad (Ferris Wheel).

Bakery Museum • 112

Piarist Church of Maria Treu • 112

Palais Liechtenstein, the Museum of Modern Art • 112,113

Josephinum • 113

The Sigmund Freud-Haus • 113

Ulrichsplatz • 112

Spittelberg • 111, 112

Linke Wienzeile • 109/111

Sezession • 108

The Naschmarkt, the Majolikahaus • 110, 111

Künstlerhaus • 107

The Karlskirche • 104, 105

Karlsplatz • 105

Karlskirche (Church of Saint Charles Borromeo) - Karlsplatz - **Historisches Museum der Stadt Wien** (Historical Museum of the City of Vienna) - Musikvereinsgebäude (Society of the Friends of Music Building) - Künstlerhaus (Artists' House) - Historische Stadtbahnstationen (Historical Underground Pavilions) - **Sezession** (Sezession Building) - Akademie der Bildenden Künst (Academy of Fine Arts) - **Linke Wienzeile** - Theater an der Wien - Naschmarkt - Flohmarkt (Flea Market) - Majolikahaus - Spittelberg - Barockhaus am Ulrichsplatz - Bäckereimuseum (Bakery Museum) - Piaristenkirche Maria Treu (Piarist Church) - Palais Liechtenstein - Museum für Moderne Kunst (Museum of Modern Art) - Josephinum - Sigmund Freud-Haus.

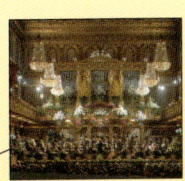

Society of the Friends of Music building • 106, 107

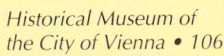

Historical Museum of the City of Vienna • 106

Historical Underground Pavilions • 107

The Academy of Fine Arts • 109

Theater an der Wien • 109, 110

The splendid white Karlskirche.

KARLSKIRCHE

In 1713, Vienna was devastated by the plague for the seventh time. Thousands of the city's inhabitants were struck down by the terrible epidemic. Emperor Karl VI, worried over the fate of the city, vowed to raise a church in honor of Saint Charles Borromeo. In 1716, after the plague had been eradicated, the architect J. B. Fischer von Erlach commenced execution of the project, which was completed after his death by his son Joseph Emanuel. The Church of Saint Charles Borromeo is considered a masterpiece of Baroque religious architecture. Seen from the man-made lake where there stands the beautiful but somewhat inadequate sculpture by Henry Moore, *Hill Arches* (1977), the exterior of the church surprises us not only on account of its imposing size but also due to the multiplicity of artistic elements that go to make up the building as a whole.

Facade - Two low, heavy towers with large open portals flank the facade. The center staircase, with a statue at each side, leads to the classical six-columned porch behind which the main door opens; on the tympanum, a stucco relief by J. Stanetti shows the *Extinction of the Plague*. The two triumphal columns at the left and the right of the church are the most surprising architectural element in the entire complex: the rich decoration, similar to that of Trajan's

Column in Rome, narrates the life of Saint Charles Borromeo, and two elegant lanterns crown the summits. The entire construction is dominated by the dome, 72 meters in height.

The **interior** of the church, on an oval plan and in large part realized in marble, is striking thanks to the harmony and the symmetry of the forms and the masterly play of the light created by the large windows of the dome.

The *high altar*, built to J. B. Fischer von Erlach's design, with its imposing scenario of gold- and stucco-work, is fascinating. The most capable artists of the time collaborated on the altarpieces: Daniel Gren, Jakob von Schuppen and Sebastiano Ricci. The fresco in the vault of the towering dome, representing Saint Charles Borromeo, supported by the Virgin as he prays for deliverance from the Plague, was painted between 1725 and 1730 by J. Michael Rottmayr.

KARLSPLATZ

This vast tree-lined square, a short distance from the Ring and linked to the center by the Kärtnerstrasse, is one of the most significative in Viennese culture, besides being an important city traffic node. Saint Charles' Square is a park with pools and monuments (of note that dedicated to **Johannes Brahms**) and is overlooked by private and institutional buildings that played important roles during the period of Vienna's artistic flowering (19th and 20th centuries).

These buildings, together with the Karlskirche, bear witness to the splendor of the former Hapsburg empire.

If we stay to the right leaving the church, we come to the Historical Museum of the City of Vienna, across from the Künstlerhaus and the Musikverein, as well as to the pavilions of the old underground stations. If we instead turn to the left in the square as we leave the church, toward Wienzeile and the Naschmarkt, we will come to the Sezession, stronghold of the Viennese Jugendstil.

Sculpture by Henry Moore in Karlsplatz.

The monument to Brahms in the Resselpark.

HISTORISCHES MUSEUM DER STADT WIEN

The Historical Museum of the City of Vienna, inaugurated in 1959, offers the occasion to make the detailed acquaintance of the history of the city and its development. Subdivided among the three floors of this modern building are exhibits of archaeological finds and objects that tell over 2000 years of history.

Ground Floor - An overview, from prehistorical times to the 15th century. The section hosts finds and documentary evidence from the Roman garrison of Vindobona, from the Vienna of the Babenbergs and relating to the building of the great churches (for example, the plans for the Stephansdom and others).

First Floor - Dedicated to the 16th and the 17th centuries. It houses finds and booty from the wars of 1529 and 1683 against the Turks, such as suits of armor, weapons, flags and numerous other objects, among which a model of the city when its walls were still standing. There are also paintings and art objects from the 18th century.

King Rudolf I. Detail of one of the original stained-glass windows of the Stephansdom (ca. 1390).

Second Floor - Exhibit rooms of the Vienna of the 19th and 20th centuries. A reconstruction of the apartment of Franz Grillparzer in the Spiegelgasse, with its original furniture, and paintings and other works by neoclassical artists. Much space is dedicated to the Romanticists and the Jugendstil artists as well as to contemporary painters (Klimt, Kokoschka, Schiele, Hausner, Fuchs, Lehmden, Boeckl). There are also some plastic works by Wotruba and a model of the city in the 19th century after construction of the Ring boulevards.

MUSIKVEREINSGEBÄUDE

The Society of the Friends of Music building, raised between 1867 and 1869 from plans by Theophil Hansen, has since that time been the center of Viennese musical events. The heart of this large building, which also houses a beautiful collection of musical instruments, is the **Grosse Musikvereinssaal**: 51 meters long by 19 in width, the hall seats 1742 and also provides 300 listening posts. The acoustics of the hall are impeccable and its decoration is magnificent: two rows of gilded caryatids adorn the walls, the ceiling represents Apollo and the nine Muses, and from the great chandeliers sparkle a myriad of points of light; this alone is sufficient to create the resplendent atmosphere of the great events. It is from this hall that the famous New Year's Concert given by the Wiener Philharmoniker is broadcast. The orchestra is one of the world's most celebrated and the Musikverein is its official home.

Nearby the Musikvereinsgebäude is the **Künstlerhaus** (Artists' House), completed in 1868; for many years it was the official gallery of the academic artists. In clear-cut contrast with their conservative current there arose the Sezession movement, of which Klimt and others were the founders. Today, the Künstlerhaus mainly hosts important temporary exhibitions.

HISTORICAL UNDERGROUND PAVILIONS

On occasion of the building of the new U-bahn during the 1970s, the two pavilions of the Karlsplatz stations of the old underground, built by Otto Wagner at the turn of the century, were restored. These are two especially suggestive buildings in iron, copper, marble and gold that reveal a notable eye to detail. One of the two pavilions gives access to the trains of the new underground, while the other hosts a Kaffeehaus and a section of the Historical Museum. The two pavilions, together with those of Schönbrunn, Pilgramgasse, Kettenbrückengasse, Stadtpark and Rossauerlände, are beautiful examples of that Jugendstil architecture of which Otto Wagner was grand master.

Above: the Grosse Musikvereinssaal, the concert hall of the Society of the Friends of Music.
The historical underground station by Otto Wagner.

SEZESSION

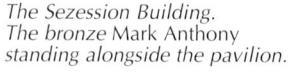

In the year 1897, a group of artists, the most important among whom were Klimt, Moser, Moll, Olbrich and Hoffmann, formed a new movement in open contrast with the academic artistic currents: it was called Austrian Sezession and its aim was to support and promote new directions in art. To this end, a new exhibit building was erected, and the Jugendstil movement elected residence there. The Sezession pavilion, built in 1897-1898, was designed by Joseph Olbrich; his is also the **cupola** of gilded iron laurel leaves that surmounts the rigidly geometric structure. The doors were built to designs by Gustav Klimt. On the facade is impressed the motto of the movement: «To Every Age its Art, to Art its Freedom». Alongside the Sezession building stands the **Denkmal der Marc-Anton-Gruppe** (Monument to Mark Anthony) by A. Strasser (1899).

The Sezession Building.
The bronze Mark Anthony standing alongside the pavilion.

AKADEMIE DER BILDENDEN KÜNSTE

Right behind the Friedrichstrasse, near the Karlsplatz, is the beautiful Renaissance Schillerplatz, with at its center the monument to the great poet. On the west side of the square is the Academy of Fine Arts building. The Academy was founded in 1692; since 1876 its headquarters have been in this building by Theophil Hansen. Vienna's is the oldest Academy of Fine Arts in the German-speaking countries and is the only one to possess a **Gemäldegalerie** (picture gallery). Here are found works by the most important artists of the 16th and 17th centuries, including Hieronymus Bosch (*Last Judgment* triptych), Cranach the Elder (*Lucretia*), Rubens (*Circumcision*), Francesco Guardi (*Eight Views of Venice*), Luca Giordano (*The Judgment of Paris*), Memling (*Crucifixion*), Pieter de Hooch (*Dutch Family*), Murillo (*Youths at Dice*), Van Dyck (*Self-Portrait*), Ruisdael (*Woodland Scene*). The collection also includes works by Tiepolo, Rembrandt, J. Miel, and many other artists mainly of the Flemish and Dutch schools. Modern-day works by Hundertwasser, Boeckl, Weiler and others are also on exhibit. The Academy also boasts an extensive **Drucksammlung** (print collection) of about 100,000 drawings, watercolors, etchings, aquatints and wood-engravings.

LINKE WIENZEILE

From the Karlsplatz, at the level of the Sezession, there begins a long roadway that leads to the Schönbrunn: the Linke Wienzeile, a popular center of city life, lined with interesting buildings. Just behind the Sezession, at No. 6, is the **Theater an der Wien**, inaugurated in 1801, where Beethoven's *Fidelio* was represented for the first time in 1805; numerous other of his works, both serious and

Theater an der Wien: the «Papagenotor» (Papageno Portal).

On these pages: No. 38 Linke Wienzeile, an example of Jugendstil architecture by Otto Wagner.

comical, were to follow. Today, mainly classical Viennese operettas and musicals are staged here. Across from the theater, on the long square that separates the left Wienzeile from the right Wienzeile, the **Naschmarkt** begins: it is a lively, colorful market where groceries, spices, exotic fruits and macrobiotic foods - in short, something for everyone - are sold. Among the shops and stalls you will also find bars and eating-places. The **Flohmarkt** (Flea Market) is held every Saturday at the end of the Naschmarkt, near the Kettenbrückengasse underground station. It is a typical bazaar of second-hand items, where among the strangest arrays of junk you can sometimes find something very interesting. But attention! If you want to dedicate some of your time to this small but very crowded market, go early: the best pieces are the first to go and late-comers are left with only useless odds and ends. The ideal spot for a pause after your visit to the Flohmarkt is the Wienzeile Café, a typical Viennese coffee-house which is always very crowded on Saturdays.

Facing the market, we can admire two splendid examples of Jugendstil architecture, both designed by the architect Otto Wagner and dating from 1898-1899. At No. 40, the **Majolika-haus**, with its majolica-tile facade in multicolor floral motifs; at No. 38, another private house decorated with gilded

medallions after a design by Koloman Moser. The balconies, the wrought-iron doors and the small columns on the facades of both buildings create an extremely ornamental effect. It is impossible to not feel the lure of such wealth and elegance, in clear contrast with the pompous style of many buildings from the same era.

SPITTELBERG

A pleasant stroll through the streets of the 6th and 7th Bezirks (Mariahilf and Neubau) leads us to Spittelberg, an old neighborhood spreading out immediately behind the Messepalast (Maria-Theresien-Platz). The Spittelberg is a low rise, in front of the ancient fortifications, that was more than once occupied by enemy armies training their artillery on Vienna, like the Turks in 1683 and the French in 1809. The 19th-century expansion of the city embraced the area, which became one of the most ill-famed, with many taverns in which dubious business was conducted. With time, the degradation reached an intolerable level: the authorities were faced with a choice - raze the entire neighborhood or re-vitalize it. Luckily, at the beginning of the 1970s it was decided to take the second line of action, implementation of which produced the results we see today: narrow alleyways with lovely, renovated houses, well-tended courtyards on which well-patronized establishments look out, excellent restaurants and crafts shops. Certain of the streets in this pedestrian area offer inviting shopping opportunities. The beautiful **Spittelberggasse**, with its various galleries, restaurants and cafés, is the heart of this neighborhood, which conceals many of its most characteristic sights in charming inner courtyards. One example is the **Amerlinghaus** at No. 8 Stiftgasse, which hosts an alternative cultural center linked to an inn. In the Burggasse, which delimits the Spittelberg area, we see the rear of the **Ulrichskirche** (Church of Saint Ulrich), built in the years 1721-1724 on the site of an oft-destroyed 13th-century chapel.

At No. 2 in the church square stands the noteworthy **Barockhaus** (Baroque House) from the mid-18th century: the richly

Courtyard of a Baroque house on the Ulrichsplatz.

The Plague Column near the Ulrichskirche.

ornate facade, the splendid courtyard, the balconies and a small pavilion in the interior lend to the whole a beauty that is rare even in a city like Vienna where Baroque homes are certainly not lacking. Crossing the Lerchenfelderstrasse and proceeding up the Lange Gasse leads us to the center of the 8th Bezirk (Josef-stadt). A beautiful Baroque house at No. 34 Lange Gasse is home to the «Alte Backstube» café where the usual connoisseurs meet, but also to the **Bäckereimuseum** (Bakery Museum). Turning down the Maria-Treugasse takes us to the Jodok-Fink-Platz, the beautiful setting for the Piaristenkirche Maria Treu.

PIARISTENKIRCHE MARIA TREU

Built in 1716 from plans by J. Lukas von Hildebrandt, the ochre facade of the beautiful Piarist Church of Maria Treu, set off by two bell-towers 76 meters in height, dominates the square. In the interior, the noteworthy *frescoes* of the dome and the ceiling, by Franz Anton Maulpertsch, represent the Coronation and the Assumption of Maria and some scenes from the Bible. The painting over the tabernacle is a work by J. Herz entitled *Maria Treu*: it was a votive offering in thanks for a miraculous recovery from the plague of 1713 and gives the church its name.

At the center of the square rises a *Mariensäule*, a work by J. Prokop commissioned by a noble in thanks to the Madonna for deliverance from the plague.

PALAIS LIECHTENSTEIN

If we go to the 9th Bezirk (Alsergrund) by car or by trolley (Strassenbahn), we will come to the Liechtenstein Garden Palace, situated between the Liechtensteinstrasse and the

Porzellangasse. Built in 1698-1711 to plans by Domenico Mar-
tinelli, it is one of the most beautiful buildings in the city. The
simple, somber facade conceals a richly frescoed interior; the
frescoes of the 27 medallions in the entrance hall, in the li-
brary, in the archives and on the staircase are by J. M.
Rottmayr; the stucco decoration is by S. Bussi and the ceiling
frescoes in the main hall are by A. Pozzo. Since 1979, this
palace has been the home of the Museum für Moderne Kunst.

Museum für Moderne Kunst - In the 15 rooms of the Museum
of Modern Art are represented almost all of the great names in
contemporary painting; that is, the great names from the time
of the Sezession through the present.
The most important section of the museum is doubtless that of
«Art of the Last Thirty Years» , in which the most novel artistic
currents are represented: Realism, Formal, Fantastic and Surreal
Art, Happening, Pop Art, Photorealism, Abstract and Geometric Art. Many of the items on exhibit belong to the Ludwig of
Aquisgrana collection. Here are collected works by such famous artists as Klimt, Schiele, Kokoschka, Kandinsky, Mondri-
an, Max Ernst, Brus, Rainer, Attersee, Picasso, Léger, Klee,
Miró, Mueller, Fuchs, Hausner, Dubuffet, Warhol, Roy Lichten-
stein, Botero - and many others.

JOSEPHINUM

Not far from the Palais Liechtenstein, at No. 25 Wahringer
Strasse, we find the 18th-century **Chirurgisch-medizinische
Akademie** in the Josephinum, built by I. Canevale in 1783-
1785. The Academy houses the **Museum des Instituts für
Geschichte der Medizin** (Museum of the History of Medi-
cine), which includes a large collection of wax anatomical
figures ordered by the Emperor Joseph II in 1775 as a learning
aid for the surgeons of the Imperial army, who often were not
sufficiently expert in providing care to wounded soldiers.
These models of the human body with exposed internal or-
gans, or accurately «skinned» in order to reveal the muscles
and the vascular system, are the work of Florentine craftsmen
(and not by chance, a similar collection is found in Florence).
The macabre melancholy of these waxen faces is at once
magnetic and highly moving.

SIGMUND FREUD-HAUS

The home of Sigmund Freud, at No. 19 on the Berggasse,
bears witness to the importance of Vienna in the field of the
modern human sciences with the **Sigmund Freud-Museum**,
which now occupies the house that the father of psycho-
analysis lived in for almost half a century. It was here that
Freud developed his revolutionary theories on the psyche and
human behavior, until in 1938, with the arrival of Hitler, he
was forced to flee Vienna.

ITINERARY VIII

OUTLYING DISTRICTS

Museum des 20. Jahrhunderts - The Museum of the 20th Century, situated in the garden in front of the Südbahnhof (South Station) was designed in 1958 by Karl Schwanzer as the Austrian pavilion for the Brussels World's Fair; following the event, it was dismantled and transported to Vienna and rebuilt on its present site. In the garden and courtyard of the museum are sculptures by Moore, Giacometti, Wotruba, Wander and Bertoni. The powerful bronze statue at the entrance is the work of Aristide Maillol (*Force Enchained*, 1905).

Heeresgeschichtliches Museum - During the 1848 Revolution, the old arsenal was attacked by the rebels; following this episode, Emperor Franz Joseph decided to build a new fortified arsenal for artillery and a weapons depot outside of the city. The result was a colossal work of military architecture, measuring 688 by 640 meters; the architects were Siccardsburg and Null, the same who designed the Staatsoper. In the interior of the arsenal was built, from plans by Theophil Hansen, the home of the Museum of Army History. Paintings,

Museum of Army History: the façade.

Heeresgeschichtliches Museum (Museum of Army History): on the facing page, a view toward the entrance hall and an exhibit of 16th-century armor. Above: the automobile of the Crown Prince, and, below, a general's «Hungarian» dress uniform.

weapons, documents, flags and uniforms breathe life into the history of the Austrian Army from the Thirty Years' War through World War I. Of particular interest, besides the grandiose exhibit of artillery pieces from the 16th through the 18th centuries, is the armor of Prince Eugene, a Turkish tent, a 1796 aerostat and the automobile in which, on 28 June 1914, Archduke Franz Ferdinand, heir to the Hapsburg throne, fell victim to the assassination attempt in Sarajevo.

Museum of Army History: 18th-century Turkish muskets.

Hundertwasserhaus - This original building in the 3rd Bezirk, at the corner of Kegelgasse and Löwengasse, is the work of the internationally famous artist Friedensreich Hundertwasser. Completed in 1985 after two years' work, this fascinating house incorporates many extravagant inventions, including the great variety of colors used and the vivaciously textured external walls with their many different kinds of windows. The multitude of plants on the roofs, the balconies and the terraces express a close relationship with nature. Not far away, at No. 13 Weissgerberstrasse, is the **Kunsthaus**, a museum dedicated to Hundertwasser and housing many of the master's paintings.

The Hundertwasserhaus and the Kunsthaus Wien.

St. Marxer Friedhof (St. Marx Monumental Cemetery): memorial to Wolfgang Amadeus Mozart.

St. Marxer Friedhof - The picturesque Saint Marx cemetery is in the Leberstrasse, in the third Bezirk, rather far from the main thoroughfares and almost suffocated by huge viaducts. It was used until the mid-19th century. Open from April to October, today it is more a garden than a cemetery, especially in May when the lilac bushes are in full bloom. It was here that in 1791 Wolfgang Amadeus Mozart was buried in the paupers' grave; his remains were never found.

Zentralfriedhof - The rapid increase in the population of Vienna during the 19th century made it necessary to build new cemeteries. The Central Cemetery, in the 11th Bezirk (Simmering) was thus inaugurated in 1874; it soon became one of the most important monumental cemeteries of Europe.

Church of the Central Cemetery (Zentralfriedhof).

Zentralfriedhof: the monumental tombs of Johannes Brahms and Johann Strauss.

From the great Jugendstil gate by Max Hegele (1905), the main boulevard leads us among secular trees to the tombs of the major personalities of Austrian culture and politics, among whom Beethoven, Schubert, Brahms, Johann Strauss father and son, Hugo Wolf, Arnold Schönberg and the Presidents of the Austrian Republic. There is also a monument to Mozart, whose burial place is the nearby cemetery of Saint Marx.

Kirche am Steinhof - This church in the 14th Bezirk, a Jugendstil master-piece, was erected by Otto Wagner in 1903-1907. Its copper dome strikes us from a distance. In designing this work, Otto Wagner omitted not a single detail: its simple and at the same time elegant lines are set off by geometric white walls, while the color gold predominates in the deco-

Kirche am Steinhof.

Kirche am Steinhof: the mosaic above the high altar.

rative motifs and portraits that embellish its interior. The *stained-glass windows* by Koloman Moser are also exquisitely beautiful.

Karl Marx-Hof - In the interval between the two World Wars, the socialist municipal government of Vienna instituted a policy of popular residential development in order to resolve the pressing problem represented by the housing shortage. Of the 64,000 apartments built in that period, a predominant part is located in the Karl Marx-Hof residential complex in the 19th Bezirk (Döbling). The more than 1300 apartments are home to over 5000 people. With its long facade (1200 meters) broken by six towers, the Karl Marx-Hof is the symbol of the so-called «Red Vienna» of the Twenties; it is considered an statement of expressionist architecture influ-

The Karl Marx-Hof.

121

The modern UNO-City complex.

enced by cubism and Art Déco. The gigantic complex, built between 1927 and 1930, is integrated by wooded areas. It was designed by Karl Ehn, a pupil of Otto Wagner.

UNO-City - This center is the symbol of Austria's neutrality and her role as mediator between East and West and North and South. The gigantic steel, glass and cement complex, situated in the 22nd Bezirk, was built in 1973-1979; in its countless offices are found the headquarters of a myriad of international organizations such as the United Nations Atomic Energy Commission, UNIDO and the Center for Social Progress and Human Rights.
Situated near the Danube and the extensive park of the same name, UNO City is composed of four buildings, 120, 100, 80 and 60 meters in height, and boasts a total of 24,000 windows.

Donaupark - This territory assigned to the 22nd Bezirk (Donaustadt), lying between the Danube and the «Old Danube», was transformed after 1964 into a beautiful park with man-made lakes, areas featuring children's amusements, skating rinks and cycle paths, all immersed in a green setting. The park also hosts the **Donauturm**, 252 meters in height, built in 1964 on the model of other television transmission towers on occasion of the Vienna International Garden Show. High-speed elevators take us to the revolving café-restaurant, 170 meters above ground level, which offers a marvelous view of Vienna and its surroundings.

In the Donaupark.

HEURIGEN

The word «Heurigen» derives from the expression «Heuriger Wein» (new wine, this year's wine) and denotes the establishments that serve this drink. These are usually found outside of the city, where the vineyards reign unchallenged, and are very often managed by the owners of the wineries themselves. The characteristic sign of the «Heurigen» is a bough of Scotch pine hanging outside. Here we can eat, drink and listen to music (above all popular music and the Viennese Lieder) in a special atmosphere that is held in high esteem by both Viennese and tourists alike. «Heurigen» are found in a number of districts within the city limits; some of the best-known are listed below.

The cosy atmosphere of the «Heurigen».

A picturesque alley in Grinzing.

Grinzing, in the 19th Bezirk (Döbling), has become famous around the world for its lantern-lit streets, its picturesque corners, its enchanted feeling. More than 30 «Heurigen» are situated here. Leaving Grinzing, the Cobenzlgasse takes us to the Hohenstrasse, which winds along the slopes of the Wienerwald (Viennese Wood), touches Kahlenberg and runs through Leopoldsberg on to Klosterneuberg. The name **Kahlenberg** is linked to the victory over the Turks by the Imperial troops, allied with the King of Poland Johann III Sobieski, in 1683. Not far from the Josephskirche (18th century), on the roof of a restaurant, is a wide panoramic terrace offering a splendid view of Vienna and the Danube valley. Another superb panorama is that from the square of the small church of **Leopoldsberg**, looking out over the Danube. The church was built in 1679 by Leopold I.

The romantic Wienerwald (Viennese Wood).

The Kahlenberg church.
Below: Beethoven's house in Heiligenstadt.

Heiligenstadt - Nussdorf - These are two more Döbling suburbs in which are situated suggestive «Heurigen» , favorite destinations for excursions. Ludwig von Beethoven lived in Heiligenstadt off and on between 1802 and 1824; certain of the houses he inhabited are still standing.

Stammersdorf, on the opposite bank of the Danube, in the 21st Bezirk (Floridsdorf), arises in the midst of the largest extension of vineyards in

The parish church of Heiligenstadt.
Below: panorama of Vienna from Leopoldsberg.

the environs of Vienna. Here are located about 100 wineries, many with their own «Heurige».

In the Hagenbrunnerstrasse, a true «Kellergasse» (street lined with wine-cellars), we are literally immersed in unique atmosphere of the «Heurigen».

Other typical establishments of this type can be found in the outskirts of the city, in Strebersdorf, Sievering, Neusift am Walde, Hernals, Ottakring, Mauer and Oberlaa (which is also a health center and spa).

INDEX